Dissenting from Donald Trump While Listening to "The Battle Hymn of the Republic"

Dissenting from Donald Trump While Listening to "The Battle Hymn of the Republic"

RODNEY WALLACE KENNEDY

WIPF & STOCK · Eugene, Oregon

Wipf & Stock
An Imprint of Wipf and Stock Publishers
199 W. 8th Ave., Suite 3
Eugene, OR 97401

www.wipfandstock.com

PAPERBACK ISBN: 979-8-3852-5184-1
HARDCOVER ISBN: 979-8-3852-5185-8
EBOOK ISBN: 979-8-3852-5186-5

VERSION NUMBER 08/12/25

Dedicated to
all "lovers of democracy"

Contents

Introduction

Mine eyes have seen the glory of the coming of the Lord:
He is trampling out the vintage where
the grapes of wrath are stored;
He hath loosed the fatal lightning of his terrible swift sword:
His truth is marching on.[1]

DONALD TRUMP BECOMING PRESIDENT of the United States shocked me. I still suffer from Post-Trump Shock Syndrome. If I had a millennium to contemplate how a congenital liar convinced a people of "truth"—the Evangelicals—to support him, I would still be confused.

His presidency has filled me with angst, a sense of resignation, and a horror of a nation ruled by conservative Evangelicals. At the same time, it has filled me with a spirit of dissent and a renewed determination to stand in the gate and proclaim the truth.

My resilient hope is this: God's truth is "marching on." Never have I so adamantly embraced the Gospel of John's affirmation, "The light shines in the darkness, and the darkness did not overcome it"[2] (I also manifest here my stubborn Anabaptist conviction, borrowed from James McClendon, that in a world without foundations, all we have is Jesus Christ and the church).

1. Howe, "Battle Hymn of the Republic."
2. John 1:5.

I confess to another layer of confusion that the Southern Baptists are leaders of MAGA and Trump. This political move flies in the face of a Baptist tradition that has never before sought a worldly foundation since they knew there is no foundation other than Jesus.

After all, I witnessed firsthand what happens when conservative Evangelicals "take over" an institution. Living through the fundamentalist takeover of the Southern Baptist Convention, I knew what happened to people of dissent. The conservatives took over and ruled every aspect of the convention, and they are still firmly entrenched in power. Some of the despair of the prophet Elijah slipped into the cracks of my battered spirit.

Dissent has always been a key word in my life, but I didn't start out to be a dissenter. Vaclav Havel, the famous poet/dissenter who became the first president of Czechoslovakia, described the way dissent comes to life. "In fact, of course, they do not usually discover they are 'dissidents' until long after they have actually become one."[3]

Dissent suggests the right of free speech and an antidote to political chicanery. As rhetorical scholar Robert L. Ivie puts it, "Dissent is the balancing point between stability and change, cleavage and consensus, politics and revolution, life and decay. It should be tolerated, not censured by authorities, punished by law, or otherwise suppressed."[4]

Dissent is the best word to describe my efforts. After all, at least one-third of the voters in the US believe Trump is "God's anointed," the "strong man," the "only one who can save us." Going against these populist views requires sustained dissent.

My role model is that poet: Vaclav Havel. In *The Power of the Powerless*, Havel gave me my motivation and purpose:

> In fact, of course, they do not usually discover they are "dissidents" until long after they have actually become one. "Dissent" springs from motivations far different from the desire for titles or fame. In short, they do not decide to become "dissidents," and even if they were to devote twenty-four hours a day to it, it would still not be a profession, but primarily an existential attitude. Moreover, it is an attitude that is in no way the exclusive property of those who have earned themselves the title of 'dissident' just because they happen to fulfil those accidental external conditions already mentioned. There are thousands of nameless

3. Havel, *Power of the Powerless*, 58.
4. Ivie, "Enabling Democratic Dissent," 46.

people who try to live within the truth and millions who want to but cannot, perhaps only because to do so in the circumstances in which they live, they would need ten times the courage of those who have already taken the first step.[5]

One of the primary emotions of dissent is anger! While I have tried hard to drain the anger from my words, the overwhelming sense of damage being done to American democracy by Donald J. Trump makes the effort less than successful. What I have written here will make some people angry—some at me and hopefully most at Trump.

Imagine, therefore, the possibility that President Donald Trump is right about everything, that he might be in a position to revolutionize all politics. Imagine that I and my fellow progressives might be able to tap our colleagues on the shoulders and tell them that we'd discovered that President Trump was making America great again and the world safer. His actions were helping solve the most difficult political conflicts in the world and would be leading us into radically new and productive directions.

That would be heady stuff—and, if Trump could really be shown to be right about everything, that's exactly what we'd do. It is our task to go where the evidence leads. So if we give the idea that Trump and MAGA are right the light of day, what will we find?

I propose we undertake an investigation with two goals. First, let's see if there is anything to MAGA claims for Trump. Let's examine the support, the reasons, the logic, and the emotions to see if there is anything of substance to the real Trump. Let's examine the politics, the religion, and the emotion behind the claims of MAGA and determine whether we are really looking at the greatest politician in world history.

If we discover the real Trump is right, we can stop right there because the reasons for the popularity of MAGA will have become obvious: MAGA is gaining support because it's correct and because it provides a new explanation of politics that exceeds traditional democratic explanations.

A great conflict with democratic orthodoxy is to be expected as the movement disposes of the nation's rotting corpse, which helps explain the trials, the accusations, and the recriminations of those on the losing side of the argument.

---

5. Havel, *Power of the Powerless*, 58.

But if this is not the case—if Trump is, in fact, a populist impostor—then our inquiry must continue because we have other questions to address. If Trump is, as his critics claim, deeply and profoundly flawed, demagogic, and destructive, as we have claimed, why has he gained such popular support? Why are Republican politicians willing to "surrender all" in loyalty to Trump? Why are Republicans willing to include in all their legislation every Trump idea, no matter how incomprehensible and dangerous? And why do a majority of the American people insist that Trump's lies don't matter and he should be followed without question? These are questions that matter, and they matter for reasons that extend well beyond the next election and even past the issue of democracy itself.

I didn't start out to write about Trump. As an American Baptist Churches USA pastor, I had plenty of work to keep me occupied. Yet the more Trump talked, the more distressed I became. The lies, the bragging, the threats, the bluster, the bullying tactics—all seemed to step on my last nerve. So I wrote an article about Trump's lies. That led to another and finally to over one hundred articles published about Trump. I also made over six thousand Facebook posts.

This literary outburst led to *The Immaculate Mistake: How Evangelicals Gave Birth to Donald Trump* and *Good and Evil in the Garden of Democracy*. *The Immaculate Mistake* makes the argument that Evangelicals had for a century been producing a character like Trump. They were not his dupes; they were his creators.

Good and Evil considers Trump as the incarnation of evil. In my study of the biblical descriptions of evil, I concluded Trump was the epitome of evil. In fact, my bias moves front and center in saying that Trump's biblical parallels reside more with the "Racha," described by Jewish theologian Andre Chouraqui:

> It is not long before we meet the Prince of Darkness on the path of wickedness. The Psalter provides him with a frightful identity card that includes no less than a hundred and twelve names, surnames, titles, and qualities. He is the very entity of evil under all its various visages. He is the opulent, the wealthy, the despoiler, the worker of sin, the man with the heart puffed up. ... He is the enemy of justice, the man oblivious to God; the oppressor, the adversary of peace. ... The father of nothingness, he incarnates a radical inadequacy and emptiness, and his works are the perfect likeness of the one who fathers them. His every word consummates a lie; his every action, a deed of violence.[6]

6. Chouraqui, "Introduction to the Psalms," 8–9.

To use Trump's own favorite rhetorical ploy, paralipsis: I'm not saying Trump is the devil, I'm just saying that he looks, talks, and acts like the devil.

Rhetorical scholars have not been kind in evaluating the rhetoric of Donald Trump. Like prophets of the Old Testament, these diligent scholars have repeatedly warned of the dangers of Trump's rhetorical strategies. Bonnie Dow says that the election of Trump threatened her teaching of the principles of rhetoric "that words matter, that reasons matter, and that rational deliberation should be central to how American culture makes decisions."[7] Paul Johnson argues that Trump's incoherent vacillations between strength and victimhood enable his white audiences to disavow hegemonic whiteness and align themselves with a marginalized, politically exiled subjectivity.[8] Robert Ivie focuses on demolition as the "guiding trope" of Trump's apocalyptic rhetoric.[9] Jennifer Wingard portrays Trump as the "product of a spoiled bunch" rather than just a "spoiled apple in the barrel."[10] Ryan Skinnell says, "Donald J. Trump is a notorious liar."[11] "Trump's rhetoric is centered on the preservation," says Michael J. Steudeman, "of a conception of American identity rooted in whiteness, masculinity, and heteronormativity."[12] Anna Young labels Trump "a populist," and Jennifer Mercieca, "a demagogue."[13] Joshua Gunn adds that Trump's political style is perverse.[14] Steudeman says, "Trump's rhetoric operates demagogically."[15] It is "centered on the preservation of a conception of American identity rooted in whiteness, masculinity, and heteronormativity. He makes sweeping condemnations of media, politicians, and public figures based on their perceived alignment with liberals."[16]

American historians have proffered the same conclusions with warnings now seen as prophetic with each new outrage of the Trump administration. David L. Blight observed, "American democracy is in peril and nearly everyone paying attention is trying to find the best way to say

7. Dow, "Taking Trump Seriously," 136.

8. Johnson, "Art of Masculine Victimhood," 8.

9. Ivie, "Trump's Unwitting Prophecy," 708.

10. Wingard, "One Bad Apple," 42.

11. Skinnell, "What Passes for Truth," 82.

12. Steudeman, "Demagoguery," 8.

13. Young, "Fear and Loathing," 25; Mercieca, *Demagogue for President*, 24.

14. Gunn, *Political Perversion*, xi.

15. Steudeman, "Demagoguery," 8.

16. Steudeman, "Demagoguery," 8.

so. Should we in the intellectual classes position our warnings in satire, in jeremiads, in social scientific data, in historical analogy, in philosophical wisdom we glean from so many who have instructed us about the violence and authoritarianism of the twentieth century? Or should we just scream after our holiday naps?"[17]

Timothy Snyder, Yale University history professor, penned *On Tyranny* as a warning against the ideology of Trump. Snyder rightly sees the dangers of tyranny, authoritarianism, and fascism: "We might be tempted to think that our democratic heritage automatically protects us from such threats. This is a misguided reflex. In fact, the precedent set by the Founders demands that we examine history to understand the deep sources of tyranny, and to consider the proper responses to it. Americans today are no wiser than the Europeans who saw democracy yield to fascism, Nazism, or communism in the twentieth century. Our one advantage is that we might learn from their experience. Now is a good time to do so."[18]

James Kloppenberg's history of democracy, *Toward Democracy*, traces the historic struggle of democracy between agonism and antagonism, between democratic principles and populism. He shows that the present problem is the Trumpian bent "to frame disagreements as all-or-nothing struggles between good and evil, between freedom and oppression,"[19] instead of seeing that democracy requires a multiplicity of voices, a powerful public space for dissent, endless negotiation, and compromise between competing values.

There's not a single good reason for disputing any of these markers of Trump. Rather, I gather all these critiques into one tropological rotten barrel of apples and extend these assertions to a basic claim: Donald Trump is a secular revivalist, evangelical preacher who traffics in evil, flaunts evil, and makes evil appear good. As Isaiah lamented, "Ah, you who call evil good and good evil, who put darkness for light and light for darkness, who put bitter for sweet and sweet for bitter!"[20] I argue that an embodied evil lies at the heart of Trump's personhood. He is a secular evangelist preaching a gospel of revenge.

I have not found a better visual metaphor of Trump than the strange preacher, Haze Motes, in Flannery O'Connor's *Wise Blood*. Motes

17. Blight, "'Lost Cause' Myth."
18. Snyder, *On Tyranny*, 13.
19. Kloppenberg, *Toward Democracy*, 17.
20. Isa 5:20.

thunders from his pulpit, "I'm going to preach a new church—the church of truth without Jesus Christ Crucified. It won't cost you nothing to join my church. It's not started yet but it's going to be."[21]

Trump, like Motes, has given Evangelicals a religion without a cross, a religion that accepted all the gifts the devil offered Jesus during the temptation. And there is the danger: a secular, faithless evangelist upheld by an evangelical faith run aground.

The air we breathe is polluted by the tsunami of Trump's hateful, vengeful, divisive, harsh, demeaning, and violent rhetoric. He has unleashed a primal anger not even he can control. The political alienation, demagoguery, violence, and advancing authoritarianism are shaking the foundations of our democracy. Dana Milbank warns Trumpism has broken away from "good-faith participation in the democratic process."[22]

Trump's nihilism exudes a bad-boy ethos, what Prusa and Brummer dub a "destructive spirit of anarchy and chaos," and what Robert L. Ivie calls a kind of "salvation by demolition."[23] Mary Stuckey says Trump ravages democratic norms and values, undermines civic culture, and inhibits deliberation.[24]

The evangelical commitment to Trump put me in a time of mourning. My people, the Evangelicals, had accepted all the gifts and promises and lies of a man I considered to be a child of Satan. What really agitated my mind was the possibility that my commitments as a scholar and a preacher were threatened. Why? Because I teach and preach the necessity of searching for the truth. I live by the conviction that truth matters, reasons matter, evidence matters, and that the truth should be central to how we conduct our nation's affairs.

No one in my lifetime has ever demonstrated such a lack of respect for the truth like Trump. He communicates through what he has called "truthful hyperbole." His speeches fill with untruthful and incoherent claims. My mind still seizes at times when I think that over 80 percent of Evangelicals have consistently supported Trump, having voted for him three times.[25]

Now, eight years later, I am more disturbed by Trump than ever. I put together this collection of my brief essays about Trump as a way

21. O'Connor, *Wise Blood*, loc. 492.

22. Milbank, "GOP Is Sick."

23. Prusa and Brummer, "Myth, Fiction, and Politics," 1; Ivie, "Trump's Unwitting Prophecy," 708.

24. Stuckey, "American Elections," 667–94.

25. Smith, "White Evangelical Voters."

of continuing to dissent from his evil ways. I have a sense that I am not doing enough to counter Trump's anti-democracy movement. Like the American historian David L. Blight, I believe the time has arrived for us to sing, to scream, and to fight (nonviolently, of course). And with the skill set I have honed over sixty years of writing sermons, I have taken up my pen to write in dissent of the ways of Trump.

The essays in this book are distilled moments of dissent, artillery blasts into the night sky. Without apology, there are ethical and emotional proofs as I incorporate Aristotle's entire rhetorical arsenal of logos, pathos, and ethos to assail Trump's ideology. My hope is the reader will feel the angst I feel and recognize the danger Trump represents. Originally printed in *Baptist News Global* as analysis pieces, the essays are in no particular order, but each one represents dissent from Trump. After all, the purpose of an opponent is to oppose.

The essays have been previously published at www.baptistnews.com, now republished here with permission. My editor at Baptist Global News, Mark Wingfield, has carefully and diligently guided my writing and has been gracious in publishing my efforts. The essays lack some of the traditional characteristics of published works. Written more in the style of the newspaper, they include one-sentence paragraphs—an accommodation that might drive English professors to heavy drinking. Each essay represents my attempt to show the rhetorical disorder of Trump. His political agency can't be ignored. His rhetorical excess has unleashed long-hidden fears, anger, and resentment in almost half of the population.

Dissenting from Donald Trump While Listening to "The Battle Hymn of the Republic"

I have read a fiery gospel, writ in burnished rows of steel:
"As ye deal with my contemners, so with you my grace shall deal;
Let the Hero, born of woman, crush the serpent with his heel
Since God is marching on."
He has sounded forth the trumpet that shall never call retreat;
He is sifting out the hearts of men before his judgment-seat:
Oh! be swift, my soul, to answer Him! be jubilant, my feet!
Our God is marching on.[1]

P RESIDENT DONALD TRUMP, AT his smirking, scoffing, bragging best, spent his State of the Union address making a campaign rally speech. He could not conceal his rage at the Democrats who are duly elected members of Congress but will not bow before him like the Republicans who spent the evening applauding, enjoying, and relishing the president's personal vendetta.

Trump believed he had every right to attack the Democrats as he laid out his plan to dismantle democracy, destroy the environment, and wreck the federal government. His cruelty was everywhere in full dress parade. His adoring fans enjoyed and applauded the cruelty.

1. Howe, "Battle Hymn of the Republic."

1

I gave the president the benefit of paying close attention to his rhetoric and facial expressions. One phrase told the story of his purpose: "These people."

Here is an example:

> This is my fifth such speech to Congress, and, once again, I look at the Democrats in front of me and I realize there is absolutely nothing I can say to make them happy or to make them stand or smile or applaud. Nothing I can do. I could find a cure to the most devastating disease, a disease that would wipe out entire nations or announce the answers to greatest economy in history or the stoppage of crime to the lowest levels ever recorded, and these people sitting right here will not clap, will not stand, and certainly will not cheer for these astronomical achievements. They won't do it no matter what. Five, five times I've been up here. It's very sad. And it just shouldn't be this way.[2]

Here's another:

> So while we take out the criminals, killers, traffickers and child predators who were allowed to enter our country under the open-border policy of these people, the Democrats, the Biden administration—the open border, insane policies that you have allowed to destroy our country—we will now bring in brilliant, hard-working, job-creating people.[3]

An Ancient Phrase

"These people" belongs to an ancient rhetoric of superiority, a phrase of division, disdain, and dismissal.

"Those people"—that's what the segregationists said about African Americans marching across the Selma bridge for the right to vote.

"Those people"—that's what nativist Americans say about brown-skinned immigrants.

"Those people"—that's what gated community, high-brow, rich people say about ordinary Americans in the rural South.

I understood exactly what Trump meant when he sneered, "These people." I grew up with those words branded on my consciousness. "Those rednecks" haunted my first three decades of life.

2. Time Staff, "Speech to Congress."
3. Time Staff, "Speech to Congress."

Trump managed to wrap all the derision and demonization of Democrats into a single phrase that previously had the decency to die in what was becoming a more diverse and inclusive America. But Trump has disinterred this discredited phrase and constructed a wall between the "superior people"—the moral, high and mighty people, God's people—and "these people."

This speech had been in the making for years. Trump keeps grudges in a fiery furnace of his subconscious and stokes the fires of his resentment as his daily prayers. And in the most inappropriate setting, with the most disgusting rhetoric and the most awful performance ever given by a United States president, he disrespected his fellow Americans.

Throwing Bombs and Making Promises

The highly partisan speech promised his supporters the moon. The lapdog Republicans were giddy at the idea of starving children, increasing the devastating impact of global warming and dismantling the "swamp."

The apocalyptic mood pervaded a deeply divided House as the "mercurial and easily offended provocateur,"[4] as the New York Times' Peter Baker described Trump, threw rhetorical bombs in head-spinning gyrations in both policy and politics. Imperialism ("We are taking the Panama Canal" and Greenland "one way or another"), nationalism, xenophobia, and sexism ("only two sexes") were the galloping horses of the apocalypse.[5]

For a teacher of speech, Trump's rhetoric was hard to endure. Rhetorical scholar Bonnie Dow has described Trump's rhetoric earlier as "coarse, indecorous, and unapologetic."[6] Robert L. Ivie, professor emeritus of rhetoric at Indiana University, argues that Trump's "hyperpolarizing misdirection of public discontent subverts democratic values and processes."[7] And Trump's open and willing reduction of Democrats made clear we are in for a long and protracted four years.

The speech was pure, undiluted Trump. The demolition motif, the rage, the disgust, the tattered bag of lies spilling out over the audience, were a vindication for Trump. As he taunted Democrats for daring to

4. Baker, "How Trump Has Reshaped."
5. Time Staff, "Speech to Congress."
6. Dow, "Taking Trump Seriously, 136–38.
7. Ivie, "Trump's Unwitting Prophecy," 708.

put him on trial, he growled, "Yeah, how did that work out for you?"[8] He forgets he is still a convicted felon and a serial liar.

His speech was riddled with lies and misinformation only a Republican Congress and a Trump rally crowd would swallow whole.

The trumpet blast signaling the tone of the entire speech, though, was "these people."

In the ancient Hebrew book of Leviticus, there is an occasion where a trumpet blows and God's *yabal* (jubilee) takes place. The *yabal* signals the breaking of the vicious cycles of competitive stealing, lying, and cheating. All the debts are forgiven, and all the wealth is distributed. The poor get their stuff back.

Trump's trumpet blast debuted the opposite of jubilee. Instead of sharing, there is going to be more for the wealthy. The president even hawked his proposed "five-million-dollar gold card" for other wealthy people to join him in America as hogs at the trough. The anti-immigration, nativist president wants to sell "gold cards" because everything is transactional. He's a phony real estate developer and a con artist. Trump will sell anything, buy anything, and he will cheat you.

With the reverse, with the "these people" comments, there's no more posturing, pretending. We are in a political war with an energized right-wing base willing to destroy democracy to "stick it to the libs." For the first time in my life, I believe it is 1861 again.

The speech seemed like an end in itself; its finger-pointing and scapegoating were classic demagogic gestures.

Trump didn't come to address the state of the union; he came to further divide us. This was classic demagoguery, meant not to advance democratic deliberation and cooperation but to shut it down with scapegoating, oversimplifying complex issues, and projecting an authoritarianism built on fear and hatred.

The Warning

Here's the warning: "these people" are Trump's fellow Americans. To us and to all humans belong the promise of our Declaration of Independence—"all men are created equal."

"These people" are the ones dedicated to the proposition of making the words of Thomas Jefferson more than an ideal, but a reality.

8. Time Staff, "Speech to Congress."

"These people" have been busy making sure "all women" are created equal, "all races" are created equal, all humans regardless of gender, color, or religion are created equal. Trump has been blinded by his own rage and publicly divorced himself from all "these people." We are no longer fellow Americans. Instead, we have been called out, branded, and identified as the enemy of the people.

I Don't Hate Donald Trump

MY CRITICS SWEAR I hate Donald Trump. Set the record straight: I do not hate Donald Trump. After writing two books opposing his rhetoric and actions—*The Immaculate Mistake* and *Good and Evil in the Garden of Democracy*—and more than six hundred articles, I have never felt an ounce of hatred. I simply don't like Trump.

In a snarly mood, I would be tempted to say I "love" Trump the way Franklin Graham loves gays. He "loves" gays but thinks they are going to hell. But that is an understanding of love foreign to my heart.

Like Sam of "I don't like green eggs and ham" fame, I don't like Donald Trump. I can't take him on television, at a live rally, on the radio, in person, in the White House, or outside Trump Tower. I do not like him.

I usually find liking people a cheerful and easy task. After all, I am a trained minister. The church and seminary taught me to be nice. I have expended a lot of energy attempting to like everyone, but I don't like Donald Trump.

My people like Trump. I grew up in Union Parish, where 73.2 percent of voters cast ballots for Trump.[1] I don't understand why so many of my relatives voted for a bullying, blustering, bragging, loudmouth reality television star. I have been fretting over this reality for eight years.

My wife says I should tell somebody. Here lately, worry and anger over this mess takes over a percentage of my sleep right off the top. So, I'm telling you, OK?

---

1. CNN, "Louisiana General Election."

6

A Little League coach, old school borderline abusive, screamed at a group of eight-to-twelve-year-old boys, "This is my team, and you will do as you are told. You are a bunch of losers. You are slow, fat, out of shape, and you can't play. Nobody in this league respects you. Your parents can barely stand to watch you on the field. You are going to shape up, and you are going to become real ball players. You are going to run until you drop. And if you don't like it, you can take your glove and go home."

All the kids, heads hanging to the ground, remained stuck to the bench in horrified silence. Except one twelve-year-old boy. He slowly stood up, picked up his glove, walked out of the dugout, climbed over the fence, and went home. We never saw him on the baseball field again. Some people don't like being yelled at and degraded.

The story returned from my subconscious history because I am sick and tired of listening to one of our politicians rant and rave about what a loser America is. I have never heard a president or ex-president talk that way about our country. This is a great country, flaws and all, and among the nations, it is the greatest country.

America doesn't need to be made great again. America only needs to embrace its potentialities and release its vast emotional energies of empathy, generosity, and concern for others, along with its imaginative and creative scientific spirit. A greater America is a good which would make all nations stronger. Just stop telling me we are a bunch of losers.

Bottom line, I'm not sure we will ever finish with all that mess about Trump's lies, sordid affairs, impeachments, insurrection, vulgar and profane language, and awful policies. Even if Trump is pissing on the Constitution, repudiating the Republic, and getting away with all his crimes, those are not the primary reasons for my refusal to support him. I don't like loudmouth bullies.

I tend not to pay attention to preachers or politicians going on and on 'til judgment day with the constant repetition of messages of fear and the good old days. I'm OK if President Biden pardons Trump for all his manifold wickedness. I just can't listen to the man.

One summer Saturday night when I was seventeen years old, I dressed for the revival service at Antioch Baptist Church. The guest evangelist had been preaching every night for six nights, and I knew Saturday night he would preach on hell. This marked the last time I ever would willingly enter a church to be told what an awful sinner I was and scared into thinking I was going to die at any moment and go to hell.

For years, I had resented the endless parade of excessively loud—in voice and clothes—uneducated reverends screaming at me. With their rolled-up black leather King James Bibles, they punctured the air like aging boxers desperate to land one knockout punch.

On this Saturday night, the preacher would have no idea why I was grinning up at his twisted, tortured face, no idea I'd made up my mind never to suffer through another of his meaningless, meandering hellish sermons.

Such sermons were, in my mind, worthless, of no use to any one as they grew up into forty-five-minute sermonic explosions of divisive phrases, hyperbole, and untruthful and often incoherent claims, attempting to whip the crowd into a fearful frenzy, leaving us no choice but to thunder down the aisle to grasp the preacher's hand and be saved from the certainty of a sure hell before dying like grass in the relentless hundred-degree heat of August. The sermon withered there on the vine, living out its dying gasps of a desperate preacher pleading, "One more verse of 'Just As I Am' to keep some poor young soul from the pits of hell."

I took my seat on the back pew, left side, with the rest of the teenage boys of our country church. None of us was thinking of hell. We were thinking of beer, rolled cigarettes, catfish, purple hull peas cooked in bacon, and girls—always girls.

It had been branded into my brain: "Before this time tomorrow I may be on my way to glory." The preacher had endlessly suggested I might have a wreck in the one mile between the church and my house, die in the flaming wreck, and go to hell because I had turned down my last chance to get saved. Never mind I had made the trek down the aisle every summer for five years because I would feel badly for the preacher because nobody was "getting saved." I no longer believed the car wreck story.

I don't begrudge those souls still fretting over hell. I quit the belief fifty-seven years ago. I believe I'm covered by blessed assurance. I've been fretting over this for all these years. I've never really credited any type of hell as an eternal destination. There's too much hell here and now and not enough good Christians doing all they can to make it less hellish.

I just don't tolerate preachers or politicians telling me I'm a loser, or sorry, or that nobody respects me.

Perhaps I am merely bored by speakers who only have one stump speech. Trump has been saying the same awful thing for eight years. He can't stop yapping about the border, the immigrants, the losers, the crazy people, the sick people, or how awful our country is. So, I've stopped listening.

Trump is a bullying Little League coach. Trump is a hellfire and damnation preacher. Trump is a boring politician characterized by harsh words, violent imagery, and scary language. I tried to like him for the sake of all my first, second, and third cousins who asked me to give him a chance. I've read his speeches. I've watched him at his rallies, in his televised appearances, his inaugural address, and his January 6 speech. They all sound the same. I don't like him.

There. I told you. You deserved to know. I feel better. Thank you.

MAGA Contradictions on the Poor and the Immigrant

W HEN PRESIDENT DONALD TRUMP canceled US grants distributed through church charitable organizations, Phil Vischer posted on X, "The Trump admin sent notices on Wednesday to the Christian orgs that work to help refugees resettle in the US—informing them that all of their contracts have been cancelled. The 45-year-old program, launched by Reagan with broad bipartisan support, is apparently finished. Trump has also canceled contracts for the emergency food supplement the US makes for kids too malnourished to eat normal food. 300,000 servings are now stuck in Georgia. Doctors fear thousands of kids will die as a result."[1]

The responses he drew from evangelical Christians and other MAGA supports on X were astounding:

- "Good, they were aiding and abetting the invasion of our country to displace us and turn the entire country Democrat/communist, whether they knew it or not. We won't be forced to finance our own replacement. Trump is finally putting an end to it."[2]

- "Awesome. That's what I voted for."[3]

---

1. Vischer, "Trump admin."

2. Steve Pender (@StevePender), "Good, they were aiding," Mar. 1, 2025, comment on Vischer, "Trump admin."

3. Haunted Humor (@bagginsbaggs), "Awesome," Mar. 4, 2025, comment on Vischer, "Trump admin."

- ◆ "And rightly so when it has been to abused to the point of driving our nation into bankruptcy."[4]

- ◆ "I haven't see any Trump supporter anywhere cheering on someone's death. Clearly I care for others. But I always consider as well that Jesus had this interaction. Seems relevant to what you're saying. Lots of suffering in life."[5]

- ◆ "You forsake our own people for strangers and criminals. As a Christian, we will care for our families. You call evil good and good evil. Snake in the grass."[6]

- ◆ "Says the side that cheered on the abuse J6 victims received not to mention the absolute euphoria they feel fighting to end baby's lives in the womb."[7]

In response, Vischer later reposted a comment from New Testament theologian Laura Robinson: "I have no idea what to do with a Christian who responds to news of starving kids with celebration. It's like there's more than one religion called Christianity and one is the perfect inverse of the other."[8]

The explosion of responses on X demonstrates a MAGA evangelical detachment from the Bible, the New Testament and the teachings of Jesus, the history of the church, and reality. In what Christian world do Christians celebrate the closing of agencies designed to help immigrants and the poor? Apparently, that would be the evangelical world of MAGA.

For Christians to support the defunding of Christian organizations, including evangelical organizations, that serve poor and marginalized people at home and abroad is absurd. But we live in absurd times when lies pass for truth and opinions pass for knowledge.

4. Ben Zeisloft (@Ben Zeisloft), "Praise God," Mar. 1, 2025, comment on Vischer, "Trump admin."

5. Jim Pfaff (@jimpfaff), "I haven't see," Mar. 3, 2025, comment on Vischer, "Trump admin."

6. Sleepy Lagoon (@SleepyLegoo), "You forsake," Mar. 3, 2025, comment on Vischer, "Trump admin."

7. Best Decade Ever (@ZachFOCO), "Says the side," Mar. 3, 2025, comment on Vischer, "Trump admin."

8. Robinson, "I have no idea."

What They Wanted

In Trump, Evangelicals got the president they always desired. As Robert Jeffress famously put it, "I want the meanest, toughest SOB I can find."[9]

As a result, Evangelicals are on a path to being Trump's tools—a path leading away from the evangelical commitments to the gospel of Jesus.

David Frum noted, "If conservatives become convinced that they cannot win democratically, they will not abandon conservatism, they will abandon democracy."[10] I think Frum is only partially right. MAGA Evangelicals will abandon even Jesus, while still saying, "Lord, Lord!"

Refusing to see the values of diversity, openness, and inclusion as Christian values, they conflate secular values with progressive values in opposition to both.

The MAGA evangelical response to Trump canceling the contracts of church agencies helping immigrants and the poor has the feel of tearing down the fences to protect the cattle from predators.

In Their Own Words

Beyond analogies, there are hard facts showing the detachment of MAGA Evangelicals from reality. I read more than two hundred and fifty responses to Vischer's social media posts, and here are the themes that sound like the chorus of a bad praise song over and over.

No More Foreigners

MAGA Evangelicals are more concerned about immigrants than abortion. Their responses towards immigrants may be summarized as not even being interested, as not seeing the contract cancellations as a problem, as immigrants being too expensive a problem for America to handle, and as a sense of total rejection of immigrants overall with a biblical dash of "Am I my brother's keeper?"[11]

The best biblical character I have found to help me understand MAGA Evangelicals is Jonah. Here's a preacher who preached a sermon and the entire city of Nineveh was converted. But Jonah was not happy.

---

9. Lyons, "Robert Jeffress."
10. Frum, "Exit from Trumpocracy."
11. Gen 4:9.

Jonah's absurd performance in the final act of the book—a Jewish comedy in my reading—is one of contempt for God's mercy for foreigners. MAGA Evangelicals play Jonah to the hilt.

Seeing Corruption Everywhere

And then there's a MAGA perception that church charities are nothing but fronts for corruption. The church is seen as aiding and abetting the "deep state." Progressive ideas of a social gospel involving the government are trashed. The important move here, according to MAGA responses, is a crackdown that follows the law to the smallest detail. In short, MAGA opposes the use of government funds for foreign aid.

For Trump and MAGA, there's corruption and fraud here, there, and everywhere. Corruption and fraud hide in the deep state, which turns out to be millions of loyal, hardworking civil servants maintaining a government that works for the people.

No Care for the Poor

MAGA Evangelicals have created an impossible situation. They claim to care about the poor, but they are opposed to the government helping the poor. And they don't give enough of their money to churches and church-related organizations to help the poor. MAGA Evangelicals perceive Christian organizations as traitors to the gospel: they are doing the work of Caesar, not of Christ. This attitude fits with the usual evangelical suspicion of government aiding the church in any area of life.

Here are a couple examples of the kinds of things said on this anti-government theme:

- "Thank God. Our government has used billions of dollars to buy off church denominations and get them to bend the knee to the culture of the day. All without the parishes knowing this was going on at this huge scale."[12]

- "Not our problem. America can no longer afford to solve the world's problems."[13]

12. Anthony (@man_of_renown), "Thank God," Mar. 2, 2025, comment on Vischer, "Trump admin."

13. Zamster (@ZamsterCrypto), "Not our problem," Mar. 2, 2025, comment on

What's Missing

George Lakoff offers a reality check on the role of the government in *The Political Mind*. The ethics of empathy shapes government. "Behind every progressive policy," Lakoff reminds, "lies a single moral value: empathy, together with responsibility and strength to act on that empathy."[14]

Government Has a Moral Mission

President Franklin Roosevelt said, "We have always known that heedless self-interest was bad morals. We know now that it is bad economics."[15]

A partnership with the government makes sense. But not to MAGA Evangelicals. They never have forgiven Roosevelt for implementing portions of the social gospel into the government. They still despise the social safety net even as they benefit from it.

Here's the problem. Evangelicals know the churches lack the money to support the national social safety net. There's too much need and too little money. By hindering government outreach, Evangelicals know they are refusing to meet human needs. They sluff it off to hating government, but what they hate is people who, in their eyes, "get something for nothing."

President Barack Obama indicated that he, like Franklin Roosevelt, understood that "when you spread the wealth around, it's good for everybody,"[16] not simply as a matter of morality but also as a practical requirement in a consumption-based economy. As historian Robert S. McElvaine argues, "Just a spoonful of socialism makes the capitalism go up."[17]

In the final analysis, MAGA Evangelicals are fighting against morality and economics.

Vischer, "Trump admin."

14. Lakoff, *Political Mind*, 47.

15. Roosevelt, "Second Inaugural Address," 53.

16. Schorr, "Wealth Gap."

17. McElvaine, *Great Depression*, loc. 855.

Forget Individual Charity

And as for the old notion that charity is up to individuals, there is this one inescapable reality: individuals can't meet all the needs of the poor, the sick, the immigrants, the down-and-out.

MAGA thinks charity is individual and church work. Nothing could be more detached from reality. The average American Christian contributes 2.3 percent of annual income to local churches.[18] There's no way the churches can meet the crushing amount of human need in the US, let alone the world.

One respondent to Vischer said that it should be parishioners who financed church charities.

Good. Let's start with your annual pledge. The two hundred dollars per year you have been pledging will need to go to twenty thousand dollars per year. You ready for that?

And Something Worse

One set of expressed feelings in the hundreds of posts left me near depression. Somehow, MAGA Christians were celebrating the actions of the administration with glee. The sense of celebration blends joy with cruelty. What if the cruelty is the point?

As I scrolled through the awful texts, I found constant expressions of joy. For example, one man was ecstatic, believing all the "fake" refugees and migrants that had been "dumped" in the US would be the next to go.

What shocked me was the complete lack of empathy. The concept of praising God for cutting off food, medicine, and supplies to the poor fails to register for me.

Any Evangelical continuing to promote the closing of church charities, the dismantling of the social safety net, the cutting of food stamps and free lunches at schools, and the canceling of contracts to help legal immigrants settle in the US should learn from somewhere they are working against the purposes of God.

18. Klein, "Average Christian Give."

Evangelicals Standing by Their Man Come Hell or High Water

(The high water pun is intentional because global warming will bring the high water and make life on earth hell)

A S THE 2024 ELECTION looms over us like a dark cloud, many Americans are fearful of the outcome. Will Donald Trump win a second term? Even asking the question has driven me to my Bible and my bourbon (Pappy Van Winkle; in a crisis of this magnitude, only the best will suffice). Will his already announced campaign of revenge against his enemies and pardons for the January 6 "patriots" become the new order?

If Trump wins, Liz Cheney warns the US could become a dictatorship. She says, "I think it's a very, very real threat and concern. And I don't say any of that lightly and frankly, it's painful for me as someone who has spent her whole life in Republican politics, who grew up as a Republican to watch what's happening to my party and to watch the extent to which Donald Trump himself has basically determined that the only thing that matters is him, his power and his success."[1]

There is one major source of consolation for lovers of democracy. According to the demos, the numbers, there's more than a good chance that Trump, if he somehow avoids federal prison, will lose the election—again.

1. CBS News, "Liz Cheney."

Evangelicals Will Fight for Him

But Evangelicals, having saddled the Trump stallion seven years ago, will do everything in their power to hand him victory again. The evangelical vote for Trump has been consistently above 80 percent in the 2016 and 2020 elections. The pundits are all convinced Evangelicals will "stand by their man" in 2024.

NPR says, "Most white evangelicals still support Donald Trump." *TIME* explores the subject, "Why evangelicals went all in on Trump, again."[2]

White Evangelicals are standing by their man. One clear reason: there is no one else. He is the entire evangelical strategy. He is the warrior, the strong man, the tough guy, the mafia don, the tyrant. They need Trump. They know they don't have a chance without him.

In the 2020 presidential election, 159 million ballots were cast nationwide. Those votes came from 66.7 percent of the eligible voting population of 239 million Americans.[3]

But white Evangelicals show up to vote at higher rates than nearly anyone else, even though their overall share of the US population is declining. Many Americans are notoriously irregular voters.

If evangelical support for Trump in 2024 mirrors 2020 levels, that will produce about thirty million votes for him. But if voter turnout mirrors the 2020 election, Trump will need more than seventy-five million votes to win the popular vote (Electoral College being a different matter).

That means white Evangelicals alone cannot elect a president. But they remain a large enough and reliable enough voting bloc to make a huge difference.

According to Pew Research Center, Christians account for the majority of registered voters in the US (64 percent). But this figure is down from 79 percent as recently as 2008. The share of voters who identify as religiously unaffiliated has nearly doubled during that span, from 15 percent to 28 percent.[4] In other words, there are more religiously unaffiliated voters today than there are white Evangelicals.

White evangelical Protestants account for 18 percent of registered voters today, down from 21 percent in 2008. A rising secular vote and

2. Perry, "Evangelicals Went All In."
3. Lindsay, "Electoral College Votes."
4. Kramer, "Religion in North America"; Hartig et al., "Trump's 2024 Victory."

a declining Christian vote are not good indicators for Evangelicals' preferred candidates, which are overwhelmingly Republican.

Republicans are aware of the democratic challenges they face. They have systematically engaged in efforts to undermine and invalidate the Voting Rights Act.

If you reduce the pool of eligible voters while keeping your own base enfranchised, you make it easier for your candidates to win.

Yet the numbers of eligible voters and their known preferences demonstrate that mainline Christians, progressive Christians, and the religiously unaffiliated have enough voting power to counteract the white evangelical influence. In November 2024, that would spell defeat for Trump.

If the rest of America votes with the same level of commitment demonstrated by Evangelicals, there is no way Trump can win.

Behind the Numbers

Evangelicals have underestimated the secular forces that are relentlessly advancing in the United States, threatening to make all Christian movements a redundant minority. It's not the Democrats that should keep Evangelicals awake at night. It is our post-truth secular culture.

Like the rising waters of the ocean, secularism is lapping into every corner of American life. Even churches are secular now. When you can't tell the difference between a TED Talk and a sermon, you know secularism is at home in the church.

A less religious and more racially diverse population is an ominous sign for Evangelicals.

White Evangelicals find themselves in a paradoxical moment as their overall share of the US population steadily declines. They wield outsized power in American politics because of their grip on the Republican Party.

But two long-term trends have resulted in waning numbers and cultural influence for white Evangelicals: increasing racial diversity at the same time that Americans as a whole are becoming less religious. Latino evangelical communities appear to be a growing trend driven in part by immigration patterns. Anti-immigration, wall-building American Evangelicals struggle to merge with Latino Evangelicals.

The Paranoid Style

The symptoms of the evangelical dis-ease with American culture bear all the earmarks of what historian Richard Hofstadter described in the early 1960s as the "paranoid style" of argument, a style that identifies clandestine figures haunting the body politic.

Our history shows the frequency of Americans falling into fits of paranoia. Those using the paranoid style included the anti-Masonic movement of the late 1820s, anti-Catholics in the late nineteenth century, opponents of FDR's New Deal in the 1930s, the devotees of the John Birch Society and McCarthyism in the 1950s, and members of both the White Citizens' Councils and Black Muslims in the 1960s.

Trump sells paranoia brilliantly. He is the best snake oil salesman in American history. Trump has sold Evangelicals a ticket to a new world that never will come. He has offered to take them back to the promised land—one that never existed. The old fantasy: America was great.

The New Fantasy: Trump Will Make America Great Again

Instead, he is on the verge of returning them to the wilderness in a way as severe as their last exile after the Scopes Monkey Trial. In that era, the preaching of Harry Emerson Fosdick and the satire of a newspaperman from Baltimore, H. L. Mencken, routed the Evangelicals. They entered a self-imposed exile of more than the biblical forty years but with the same kind of devastating results.

Four Factors Against Evangelicals

I am convinced several factors are working against the evangelical ability to win the 2024 election for Trump.

First, eternally optimistic Americans—why else do we buy so many lottery tickets?—will not long abide in the land of fear, paranoia, anger, and disgust. Hopefully sooner rather than later, the exodus of Evangelicals from the fake world of Trump will become a horde of immigrants retreating into reality.

Second, Evangelicals can be their own worst enemies. They have skills, acquired over many battles, that work against the success of their movement. For example, Evangelicals are more likely to reduce the size of the circle of inclusion.

With militant, zealot-like determination, Evangelicals have locked down their small circle, closed the border, and posted guards authorized to allow admittance only to the godly.

Third, Evangelicalism is now rooted in turning away from good faith participation in the larger community of faith. The ensuing politics of polarization and authoritarianism destroy any hope of ecumenical cooperation in discovering truth, decency, unity, racial progress, and academic expansion.

Fourth is the dreary conformity of the evangelical movement. The evangelical beating heart involves a fantasy of atomism, an unhealthy dogmatic contrarianism. In the Monty Python movie *Life of Brian*, the crowd repeats, "We're all individuals."[5] Evangelicals think they are being courageous, radical, and different all by being exactly the same as each other.

Evangelicals are once again becoming what they always have been: a minority voice. They control what they control—some denominations and one political party—with an iron grip, a collection of private Christian academies and universities, and an array of conservative think tanks. They console themselves with Fox News as they stare inevitable defeat in the face.

Who Will Show Up to Vote?

All the factors mentioned are related to the demos of registered voters in the US.

In the play-up to "November Madness," what matters is how all Americans respond. We outside the cult of Trump possess the power to disrupt the evangelical juggernaut. The result of the 2024 election sits with us. Our actions will determine the outcome, not the obvious problems within evangelical faith.

We will determine the future of democracy in America in this year's election. It is now time to throw off fear and know that coming to the defense of democracy is not partisan politics; it is a spiritual necessity.

I believe the American (and Baptist) love of democratic dissent will once again rise from the ashes of authoritarianism to reassert its power.

5. Jones, *Life of Brian*.

Barabara Tuchman wrote, "A nation in consensus is a nation ready for the grave."[6]

In their wake, true lovers of democracy will rebuild shared, common public spaces. Over time, there will be a national healing and a shift to a more democratic political culture. Those presently engaged in the effort of developing an expanding circle of democratic community possess the power to take back the nation from the zealots of evangelical faith and their trained champion, Donald Trump.

Crunching the numbers offers hope, but we must fight with determined politics, with organization to increase the number of voters. Doing the hard work of democracy calls us into the streets where we must fight nonviolently. Here is a way forward for regenerating the spirit of democracy powered by the zeal of an inclusive faith.

6. Tuchman as quoted in Coffin, *Credo*, 82.

I Tried to Analyze a Trump Speech

L ISTENING TO A TRUMP rally speech is like driving in a major city with no traffic lights, stop signs, cautions, or rules. "Hammer down, pedal to the metal," demolition derby from start to finish.

Trump, long a master of not being restrained by anything, spews a NASCAR-worthy tirade of lies, exaggerations, made-up stories, incredulous claims, simplistic dualisms, and a puerile promise of salvation.

His most recent absurd broadside threatens the existence of democracy.

"I always say we have the outside enemy, so you can say China, you can say Russia, you can say Kim Jung-Un," Trump told supporters at an Aurora, Colorado, rally. "But it's the enemy from within, all the scum that we have to deal with that hate our country. That's a bigger enemy than China and Russia."[1]

He said this to cheers from his crowd.

Later, Trump told Fox Business host Maria Bartiromo, "We have some very bad people, we have some sick people, radical left lunatics. And I think they're the—and it should be very easily handled by, if necessary, by National Guard, or if really necessary by the military."[2]

Trump's public desire for an authoritarianism consolidating his power over the people has never been more clearly stated. His penchant for violence combined with his love of authoritarian tendencies is crazy beyond measure.

1. Roll Call, "Rally in Aurora."
2. Bartiromo, "Donald Trump."

Tim Walz quoted Trump's own words in a campaign speech. "Donald Trump over the weekend was talking about using the US Army against people who disagree with him," Walz said. "Just so you're clear about that, that's you. That's what he's talking about. This is not some mythical thing out there. He called it the 'enemy within.'"

The Trump campaign responded, "Tim Walz peddles a disgusting lie that President Trump will use the US Army against his political opponents: 'That's you, that's what he's talking about.' This is reckless, dangerous rhetoric. Tim should be ASHAMED of himself."[3]

Yet Trump's words are perfectly clear. Walz was not wrong.

No One Knows What to Do About Trump

The media has tried summarizing and explaining what Trump says. This has been labeled "sanewashing" by Parker Molloy, media critic and author of "The Present Age" column on Substack. This has the effect of making Trump sound better than he is.

Political scientist Brian Klaas calls Trump's speeches "the banality of crazy."[4] People are no longer mesmerized by Trump's shocking statements. He has said so many crazy things; all of Trump's craziness has become the new normal even though it is a form of language cancer spreading all over the body politic. People are now immune to Trump, numbed by crazy pronouncements like immigrants "poisoning the blood."

The present conventional wisdom seems to be attempting to give Trump the microphone and reporting everything he says. This also has a major disadvantage. Trump says so much, and his speeches are so long. The daily news cycle consists of "lite bites," and a two-hour Trump speech doesn't fit the model. The repetition alone is detrimental to one's mental health.

The announcement of Trump saying something crazy is now greeted with the words of my own saintly mother when someone showed up to tell her something about me: "What has he done now?" President Trump and his cabinet of lackeys and buffoons is a clear and present danger to our nation's democracy—a historic disaster in the making. Each day seems to bring some new violation of a moral and national red line. The president has made violating the historic principles of democracy and the

3. Haner, "Walz."
4. Klaas, "Trump Rants About Sharks."

rule of law so routine that even skimming the headlines doesn't make it possible to keep up with his missteps.

In the 2024 campaign, Trump has thrown out several vicious charges. "They are eating the cats and dogs in Springfield, Ohio."[5] Illegal immigrants are carrying diseases and have a "murderer's gene" in them. Harris is a stupid woman. Walz is a communist. If Trump loses the election, it will be the end of the USA.

When you have heard one Trump speech, you have heard them all. Using his recent rally speech in Scranton, Pennsylvania, as a model, here's what I heard. He hasn't changed his content. He's still the same racist, fearmongering demagogue he always has been. He mixes lies about immigration, taxes, and the imagined decline of America with variations on those same themes.

In some ways, he is the same now as he was in 2015, but his mood is darker. He has morphed into a full-grown, scary secular apocalyptic preacher. Trump, preaching hellfire and brimstone, has gone "Dark MAGA." In Scranton, he talked of Elon Musk being given a black MAGA cap. Trump said he didn't even know they had such a cap. But he loved Musk labeling it "Dark MAGA." Trump said, "Now I find out it's like the hottest thing going, dark MAGA."[6]

This is a truthful name. Trump always has been dark, but now the MAGA "savior of the world" has gotten darker in mood and tone.

The approach I decided to pursue was to put as much of Trump's crazy material in one place as possible with minimal interpretation. I am aware of the MAGA predilection no longer to pay any attention to Trump's words because they already have experienced "total identification" with Trump. He has a persona of a powerful, strong, brilliant leader, and no amount of craziness by the actual human being named Trump will change MAGA's vision of his persona.

I still think we are having a hard time grasping that the rhetorical dynamics swirling around Trump are characterized by a visual form of rhetorical reasoning—more about image and persona than his actual words. MAGA already has been sold on Trump by how he presented himself. He is strong; Harris is weak. He will change things immediately for the better; Harris will destroy America. He is really smart; Harris is

5. Murphy, "Truth About Springfield."
6. Trump, "Rally in Scranton."

as dumb as the rocks. The simple dualism has sealed the deal for MAGA, but the rest of us are still reeling from the obvious craziness.

An Outline of a Speech All Over the Rhetorical Map

I tried to outline Trump's speech in Scranton. He starts, as always, by bragging on the size of the crowd. Then he starts attacking: crooked, cheating Democrats; murderers pouring across our border; fake news; lying Kamala (she never worked at McDonald's); Harris having led the worst rescue operation in history; illegal immigrants coming in from everywhere, especially the Congo; back to Biden; back to illegal immigrants; his doing well in Minnesota; Harris to kill the energy industry; back to Biden; Walz the Marxist, communist; attacking the Green New Deal scam; windmills; back to the crazy Democrats; frack, frack, frack; back to immigrants and the wall; men playing in women's sports; open borders where criminals are allowed in; the assassination attempt; a coal plant in Homer City, Pennsylvania; back to North Carolina hurricane response; FEMA; electricity prices going up 100 percent under Harris; electric cars and Elon Musk jumping around at Trump rally; energy from oil production; teleprompters and Biden; Afghanistan ("We lost 13 soldiers, great soldiers. We left billions and billions of dollars behind. We left Americans behind. You have Americans right now in Afghanistan and they cannot be happy, right? They're probably—many are probably dead"[7]); the border invasion ("How about the 13,099 illegal aliens convicted of murder? They're roaming free."); Harris having lost 325,000 migrant children; inflation the worst in the history of our country; middle class to be saved and no war in Ukraine; Hurricane response again; Harris not fit to be president; Trump as tougher than all the world's dictators; stupid people running our country; a videotape of the Trump military compared to the very woke military that we have now.

After showing the obnoxious video, Trump says, "So, it's a little exaggeration. Probably, really not that much, actually."

This is a moment of honest reflection when Trump admits his exaggerations, sort of.

---

7. Quotes in the section from Trump, "Rally in Scranton."

He also says, "I must be very good as a motivator because by the time I finish my speeches, every time I'm angry as hell because I can't believe what's happening to our country, what they're doing to our country."

This is an inadvertent truthful admission that Trump's speeches are designed to increase anger among his supporters.

But He's Not Done Yet

Then Trump returns to "Kamala Harris is going to significantly raise taxes." Kamala will deliver a 1929-style depression, not a recession. Trump swears, "I will deliver lower taxes, lower regulations, low energy costs, low interest rates, low inflation and the greatest economy in the history of the world, which we had four years ago."[8]

Next, Trump plugs Steve Moore's book *The Trump Miracle* and Melania's book, along with bragging on Bill O'Reilly as a really good guy.

Then he returns to other claims: corporate taxes down to 15 percent; stiff tariffs; Trump brags on himself as he bashes America. "We are a nation in decline. We're a failing nation. We're a failing nation, and they have no clue what to do. She wants to raise everybody's taxes and what they do. You know, today, they used to go to different states. If Pennsylvania was high, they'd go to another state. But now, they go to different countries."

Trump begins winding down his almost two-hour performance with old charges: Harris is going to take away your guns; free sex changes for illegal aliens in detention; Tampon Tim; Democrats a true threat to democracy ("Tim and Comrade Kamala are really a true threat. They are a true threat to democracy. I'm not a threat to democracy. I'm the one that's going to save democracy. I'm the one that's going to save—I'm going to save democracy. They are a threat to democracy, and they really are, too. Also, you know, a big thing that's a threat is incompetence is a threat to democracy."[9])

Trump now switches from how stupid the Democrats are to how smart they are. But they are "very vicious people that have to be—you know that they are very radical left lunatics. But they are smart. In some cases, genius. Look what they could do with elections. Look what they do."

Trump claims Democrats are sick people. "These are sick people. These are bad people. And we got to beat them, and we got to beat them

8. Trump, "Rally Speech."
9. Trump, "Rally Speech."

badly, and we got to get them the hell out of there. We're going to get them out. But with your vote this November, we're going to defeat these radical left lunatics, and we're going to finish the job that we so brilliantly started."

Trump closes by offering his evangelical lovers the fulfilment of most of their dreams:

> I will support universal school choice. We will get Critical Race Theory and transgender insanity the hell out of our schools immediately. And we will keep men out of women's sports. I will defend the Second Amendment, protect religious liberty and restore free speech, and we will secure finally our elections.
>
> We will secure them. Everyone will prosper, every family will thrive, and every day will be filled with opportunity and hope. But for that to happen, we must defeat Kamala Harris and stop her radical left agenda once and for all. We want a landslide that is too big to rig. We want to have it, too big to rig.

A Brief Rhetorical Analysis of Trump's Too Many Crazy Claims

With a large brush, Trump paints a consistent picture of the dark destruction of our nation, himself as the only possible savior, Harris as a total disaster—a stupid person, incapable of solving a single problem—and the promises of him fixing everything immediately. Trump jumps from topic to topic as if his words were a dropped and burst-open bag of Mexican jumping beans.

His simplistic rhetorical strategy consists of throwing an endless number of subjects against the wall, with no attention to truthfulness, and hoping some of them will stick. His rhetoric makes deceptive promises about change. His crazy rhetoric feeds a collective fantasy that he will get things done by shaking up politics as usual. No one notices he is disrupting democracy.

MAGA will not realize Trump is lying to them as well until it is too late. His deception hinges on an undeliverable promise of national salvation, a salvation as unreal as the evangelical hopes of the rapture. They will still be thinking he is developing America into the greatest nation in the world, blissfully unaware he is using a wrecking ball to destroy the foundations of America.

Evidence, facts, truth, reality are nowhere within a hundred miles of Trump's endless variations of attacking Harris and the Democrats while constantly bragging on himself and his accomplishments—all of which are untrue.

Trump has grown older, darker, more unhinged, less organized, less coherent, and more incomprehensible in the last four years. His decline never was as evident as his performance at the town hall in a Philadelphia suburb. After two medical emergencies during the event, Trump ordered the sound technician to play Pavarotti singing "Ave Maria." He shouted, "Louder! Louder! Louder!" until he was satisfied with the volume. He did his dysfunctional version of dancing and made odd sounds as if he were televangelist Paula White speaking in tongues and summoning angels from the coast of Africa to save the 2020 election for Trump.[10]

Then Trump had his "favorites" playlist of songs entertain the audience for thirty-nine minutes. There were no more questions. There was this unexpected, spontaneous musical concert. Behind the dancing Trump, a female MAGA supporter had a strange look on her face. After about ten seconds, she rolled her eyes as if she couldn't believe what was happening.

Trump was dancing badly on a stage for thirty-nine minutes as if he were Nero fiddling while Rome burned. This is the definition of crazy.

10. Trump, "Rally in Philadelphia."

America Makes Hard Right Turn to Trump

AFTER DECADES OF PROGRESSIVE influence, America made a hard right turn on Tuesday, November 5. Donald Trump won a decisive Electoral College vote as well as the popular vote.

I resist the notion that the nation was voting against having a woman of color as our president. While I do believe gender was the dominant issue, it is not for the reasons usually assumed. I am convinced Trump's gender-performed masculinity was the key to the election.

Trump's gendered performance has two foundations: a hardcore "good old boy" masculinity and a right-wing populism dominant among authoritarian foreign leaders.

The Proverbial "Good Old Boy"

I have studied and written about Donald Trump for nine years. In this time, I never have given him enough credit for being an image and media genius.

He managed to transform himself from a city slicker into the proverbial Southern "good old boy." And he enticed more than half of America to vote for him.

"Good old boys" never have been loved before. The rest of the nation has made fun of them, caricatured them, called them "rednecks," and refused to allow them a place in polite society. Good old boys hung out in bars and bragged of sexual conquests. Good old boys could "hold their liquor," "protect the girls," and "keep their feelings private." Nobody really liked a good old boy until the New York billionaire Donald Trump became one. As frightening as this image is, it is still an act of genius—evil genius.

In the last month of the campaign, Trump doubled down on his persona as a brash, bold, bragging, "take names and kick butt" masculine savior. His torrent of words—always ugly, vulgar, divisive, harsh, violent, disgusting, and offensive—became worse. The explosion of repetitions, incomplete sentences, long rambling stories unrelated to his topic—all were intended to show Trump as the "man's man" and Kamala Harris as a weak and ineffective candidate.

This is Trump magic. Trump supporters saying, "That's just Trump being Trump," were actually saying, "Boys will be boys."

Trump, the television creature, played the role of his life: the quintessential, archetypal Southern "good old boy." And he managed this feat without drinking a single beer at the Dew Drop Inn or shooting deer or going to a drag car race.

Trump oozed the markers of the Southern good old boy: He was a fighter, a lover, and a party lover. He could claim friends in low places. He could boast, brag, lie, and preen with the best of them. Trump claims to love women but clearly demonstrates his lack of respect for women.

I am convinced a set of male performative strategies are central to Trump's campaign. Trump pretended to be hurt by the replacement of President Joe Biden with Vice President Kamala Harris, but I think his hypermasculinity relished the contest against a woman.

The first debate suggested Trump was not as cocky or confident in the face of an intelligent, tough, and beautiful woman as his rhetoric usually suggests, but his deep-seated masculine performances after the debate tell us Trump not only suffered the stereotypical insecurity of the brash male but also the tendency to fight dirty and nasty.

Masculine Rhetoric

The masculine rhetoric dominated Trump's speeches in the last month of the campaign. Nothing shouts "good old boy" like threatening people.

According to NPR, "Trump has made more than 100 threats to prosecute or punish perceived enemies."[1] He growled if "radical left lunatics" disrupt the election, "it should be very easily handled by—if

1. NPR, "Trump Threatens."

necessary, by National Guard, or if really necessary, by the military." He claims his second term will feature "retributions."

Kamala Harris "should be impeached and prosecuted," Trump said at a rally last month.

"I will appoint a real special prosecutor to go after the most corrupt president in the history of the United States of America, Joe Biden, and the entire Biden crime family," Trump said last year.[2]

Trump's rhetoric imbibed the "Lost Cause" of the South to the dregs. He managed to turn more than half of the nation into a version of "Lost Cause" ideology. This included the "Blue Wall" states of Michigan, Wisconsin, and Pennsylvania—none of which are in the South.

Trump's genius also lies in his ability to convince his followers they are being scorned by the elites. Roderick Hart has argued the real subject of the last eight years has not been Trump but the American people.

In *Trump and Us*, Hart observes, "Donald Trump knew that many Americans felt ignored, so he acknowledged them with an accessible, populist style. He knew that some folks felt trapped, and he uplifted them via emotion-filled storytelling. Others of his constituents felt besieged—by elites, especially by the media—so he offered them public therapy by becoming an alternative news source for them. Trump also sensed that many Americans were weary of the political establishment, so he used his distinct personality and a barrage of tweets to energize them."[3]

Gendered Performance and Right-Wing Populism

There also was a deeper gendered performance more dangerous than the "good old boy." Right-wing populism has introduced a maleness that undergirds political power.

This gendered performance has shown up across the globe. One can point to several leaders in other countries who have the same populist gendered performance as Trump: Viktor Orban (Hungary), Jaroslaw Kaczynski (Poland), Nicolas Maduro (Venezuela), and Narendra Modi (India) to name a few. But the two most influential right-wing populists are Vladimir Putin (Russia) and Recep T. Erdogan (Turkey).

Putin and Erdogan have managed to hide much of their political program in an "ostentatious masculine posturing that has the virtue of

2. Samuels, "Special Prosecutor."
3. Hart, *Trump and Us*, 5.

being relatively malleable,"[4] according to Betul Eksi and Elizabeth Wood. They came into power with the gendered performance of "bad boys." They posed as outsiders, as transgressors who would be hard, tough, protective fathers. They adopted "macho" approaches in their public appearances, speeches, and actions.

Both leaders produced a machismo combined with a deeper bullying, a masculine set of performances matched with a paternalistic dominance that claims to protect their own people. They successfully presented themselves as being transgressive out of necessity so they could become good fathers saving their nations by rejecting others whose masculinity they impugned by emasculating them. This combination of "bad cop" / "good cop" produced a populist authoritarianism.

Eksi and Wood demonstrate how Putin and Erdogan share a media image as the ultimate bad boys wielding their anger and macho rhetoric in defense of their nations. But they are also, paradoxically, presented as good fathers who protect those same nations.

Trump successfully mirrored the same gendered performances of Putin and Erdogan. His angry explosions over faulty microphones coupled with his gross simulation of sexual acts with the microphone was a gendered performance. His attacks on immigrants, his profanity, his declarations of how angry he was and how he would have the audio techs beaten up and how he wouldn't pay the bill for faulty equipment, his attacks on Harris, Pelosi, and women in general—all gendered performance.

Trump deliberately claimed to love women and promised to protect them "whether they like it or not." He called Harris "a shit vice president," claimed she was a "low IQ person," and attacked her as weak. At his Latrobe, Pennsylvania, rally Trump said of Harris, "She's a horrible person, but she's radical left and crazy. Bernie is radical left. And this one, Kamala, is further left than them. So you have to tell Kamala Harris that you've had enough, that you just can't take it anymore. We can't stand you. You are a shit Vice President. The worst. You're the worst Vice President. Kamala, you're fired. Get the hell out of here. You're fired. Get out of here. Get the hell out of here, Kamala."[5]

Trump won the election with this combination of "good old boy" persona and the right-wing populism borrowed from Putin and Erdogan.

---

4. Eksi and Wood, "Right-Wing Populism," 733.

5. Trump, "Rally in Latrobe."

He chose the populist image, and it became his persona. He acted the part of the "bad guy," the evil antihero, the villain as an angry, transgressive leader who would get America back on track.

He projected a nativism that castigated immigrants as deficient. He played up a male-dominated and conservative set of ideas "that appear to," argue Eksi and Wood, "restore an imagined and idealized gender order based on male dominance that will provide stability and 'greatness' to [America]."[6]

The election was not so much about a biracial woman being the Democratic candidate. It was about Donald Trump being an old-fashioned "good old boy" and a populist "bad boy." Trump gave the performance of his life—the good, the bad, and the ugly. America bought his act and elected him president.

Consider that 54 percent of Latino males voted for Trump. According to exit polls, his overall share of young males increased to 47 percent, and his share of African American males also increased.[7]

Trump's male-dominant gendered performance is an old male stereotype but was a major contributing factor in his election win.

6. Eksi and Wood, "Right-Wing Populism," 737.
7. Hartig et al., "Trump's 2024 Victory."

How Trump Won Young White Men

DONALD TRUMP WON THE 2024 election with unexpected help from young white men. Fifty-six percent of young white men voted for Trump, compared to only 41 percent of young white women.

The surprising results have led reporters to suggest several reasons for the switch from 2020 when 56 percent of young men voted for Joe Biden. Some claim social media, political apathy, and economic fatalism spurred young men to support Trump. Others suggest confused male identity. The gendered performance of Trump's "manly man" persona was appealing.

More specifically, young Gen Z white men—mainly those without college degrees—voted overwhelmingly for Trump (67 percent), which is eerily similar to their just-older millennial peers (also 67 percent).[1]

Nic Sumners, a twenty-one-year-old cosmetic car repairman from Virginia, says Trump talks about the American people in a way that resonates with him, without—in his opinion—faulting him for his gender and sexual orientation. "I'm a straight white man, and I feel like we take the blame for a lot of things," Sumners says.[2]

The cultural politics of emotion had more to do with the results of the 2024 election than policies, racism, sexism, or immigration. This election was about Trump's uncanny ability to get people to feel he was on their side as their strong protector. He bragged about being the smartest man in the world. He offered bullying suggestions to thorny foreign

1. Stanaland, "Gen Z Men."
2. Iafrate, "Why Harris Lost."

policy issues. He recently warned Hamas to release the hostages in Gaza in two weeks or "all hell will break loose."[3]

There seem to be two major reasons young white males supported Trump in 2024: masculine gendered performance, and shame and blame.

Masculine Gendered Performance

Jennifer Mercieca reminds us Trump is a rhetorical genius and a marketing genius: "Trump is probably a marketing genius; he is, essentially, whatever he can convince us to believe that he is. Some call him a con man, some call him a truth teller, and some call him a demagogue."[4] He is a creature of television, and his rhetoric and actions sound and look scripted. His use of social media attracted young white males already fans of Joe Rogan, for example.

Trump's masculine performances are more than what we hear and see on the surface. His coarse, vulgar, indecorous, and unapologetic rhetoric feeds a collective fantasy that he is a big, tough man who will get things done by shaking up politics as usual. Robert Ivie says, "His act is political theater that stymies rather than presages positive change."[5]

Mark Andrejevic observes Trump's demagogic "jouissance," which provides "a kind of pleasure in spectacle that merges entertainment with politics, skepticism with fantasy, and violence with authoritarianism."[6] Like a modern P. T. Barnum, Trump sold his supporters sheer entertainment.

Trump speaks and acts the way young white men wish they could speak and act. They feel empowered by Trump's act of sheer maleness. Trump voters often claim to hate the way he talks, the way he treats the presidency, the way he treats women and minorities, but they voted for him because of the promises he made.

Since Trump looks, sounds, and acts like a man's man, he won the admiration and votes of the majority of young white males. His caricature of a real man would be laughable if not so dangerous.

Some young Trump voters appealed to what they felt was Trump's strong belief. Tired of being shamed by feminism, young males were

3. Kelly, "All Hell Will Break Out."

4. Mercieca, *Demagogue for President*, 29.

5. Ivie, "Trump's Unwitting Prophecy," 708.

6. Andrejevic, "Jouissance of Trump," 651–52.

attracted to a male candidate proud of his masculinity. Trump became the hero for being loud, appearing strong, and saying whatever he was thinking. "We're not racist; we're not misogynistic," nineteen-year-old Coby said. "We're just normal people, and we [are] friends with everyone. We're tired of hearing a lot of this BS of the far left."[7]

There's nothing in that defense except emotions. The Trump emotion machine produces "feeling good, feeling free"[8] every day. Instead of policies, promises, or even a political philosophy, there's a certain image that Trump is strong, loud, talks endlessly, and says whatever he wants.

Trump's gendered performance was an Oscar-winning moment for young white males. His maleness undergirded his populism. His ostentatious masculine posturing won him respect. As an outsider and a bad boy but also a good father, he appealed to young white males.

Trump excited deep feelings of worth and meaning into the lives of frustrated young evangelical males. They felt they were back in control again.

This begs the question: Back from where? Trump convinced young white voters he could give them back something they had lost. This is a sort of "lost cause" philosophy for young white men.

Trump's performance included hateful, violent, and misogynistic bar talk, boasting, and bragging. He played the role of an old vision of the American male as a bootstrapping, butt-kicking, in-your-face individual unafraid to face the world.

Young white males feel they have been the "ninety-eight-pound weakling on the beach," getting sand kicked in their faces. Trump, their new daddy and protector, has shown up to put the bad guys in their place.

Shame and Blame

Young white males protest about the burden of being white in a culture they believe shames and blames them for everything.

"I feel like there's this cultural frustration that young men have that they're not allowed to be young men," says twenty-six-year-old Benji Backer from Arizona. "We feel really blamed for things that we haven't had an opportunity to impact." He added, "Well, I can't change the fact that I'm white, I can't change the fact that I'm a man, I can't change the

7. Iafrate, "Why Harris Lost."
8. Schaefer, "Whiteness and Civilization," 2.

fact that decades or centuries ago, people made bad decisions. All I can do is do what I can do now. And what I'm doing now is treating people as fairly as possible because that's what I firmly believe in."[9]

A sense of shame hangs over young white males and probably most whites, especially the previous masters of shame (conservatives), like fog on a coffin lid. Donovan O. Schaefer argues the success of Trump's rhetoric emerges in part through his mastery of a circuit of shame and dignity, in which supporters who feel ashamed find, in his verbal and visual style, a repudiation of that shame and so mobilize behind him.[10]

Trump's macho, manly man style and rhetoric matches perfectly with his ability to transform felt shame into a kind of dignity. Young white male voters refer constantly to being made to feel ashamed and blamed. Trump replaces this as he attacks "wokeness" and goes after feminism and liberalism.

There's little doubt the political left traffics in a pedagogy of shame. The civic morality of our culture teaches whites to be ashamed of past transgressions. Trump taught young white males as a preacher who offered freedom from guilt, shame, and blame with no repentance.

Trump effectively communicated to young white males that the politics of gender, race, or queer emancipation should not make them feel shame.

Schaefer points out, "In fact, we might even say that this orientation to shame is one of the cardinal principles of progressivism."[11] Progressives understand the necessity of shame, but this distinction is lost on young white males.

Feminist Elsbeth Probyn confesses, "I've been shamed by feminism. What feminist hasn't?"[12] She sees this as a positive. It is an openness to being taught a better way in the future.

Yet Trump taught young white males to see shame as a completely negative experience. Left and right political ideas diverge on the level of feelings. Being shamed, to a conservative, is something they are no longer willing to tolerate. This is a major reason young white males voted for Trump while not liking his rhetoric or his action. He freed them from shame and blame.

9. Janfaza, "We Asked."

10. Schaefer, "Whiteness and Civilization," 17.

11. Schaefer, "Whiteness and Civilization," 6.

12. Probyn, *Blush*, 75.

Voting for Trump became a way to repudiate the shame of left-wing pedagogy. Instead of shame, young white men were offered a felt sense of dignity and pride.

Young white males cared about Trump making them feel good about being men. Someone as wealthy and powerful as Trump made them feel good. This is why they were not bothered by Trump's lying or bad behavior or his criminal convictions—because he showed them he could do as he pleased, get away with it, and still be president. That puts us in jeopardy of being swamped by an authoritarian strong man who makes voters feel good. Not a good place for democracy.

Why I Keep Writing About Donald Trump

WRITING ABOUT DONALD TRUMP has been a ten-year cottage industry. Some observers say people are tired of Trump. This argument suggests writing about Trump only keeps him in the news cycle and does more harm than good. There's merit to this line of thought.

I belong to the other school of reporting on Trump. Here's why: the danger is now. That is why I still write about Donald Trump. He is the incarnation of evil flying in the robes of a hypocritical, sold-out religious group loosely identified as Evangelicals. He is a low-grade fascist, a demagogue, a renegade populist, a rhetorical pervert, a serial liar. He is a rhetorical arsonist who will not hesitate to light the fire and burn down the house of democracy.

In a July 4 message on his Truth Social platform, Trump posted an image of himself standing in front of a burning White House. This was not a scene from *White House Down* or *Olympus Has Fallen*. This was an unintended reality check on how far Trump will go to protect, not our country, but himself.

Between a Coup and an Insurrection

I cannot think of a time when I have been more upset and heartbroken than on January 6, 2021. Drinking even more coffee than usual, pacing the room, my eyes remained glued to the television as I watched and listened to President Trump incite his followers to march on the Capitol.

What he said went beyond the pale of sedition in my mind, but to his followers he was simply repeating the fact that the election had been unfairly "stolen" from him. Twenty-one times he used the word "fight." To be fair, he did use the word "peace" one time. The crowd chanted, "Fight for Trump!"

What happened can only be described as something between a coup and an insurrection. Trauma and shock made understanding impossible. When Trump finally gave in to demands from his allies to issue a statement, he gave one of his usual noncommittal statements. It was barely different from his "good people on both sides" statement after Charlottesville.

Trump, employing his favorite rhetorical trick, paralipsis, offered with one hand and took back with the other.

His mystical stereotyping, his syrupy sentimentality, spoke of loving the domestic terrorists rummaging through the Capitol building. In a video, Trump spoke of them as special people. He called them "great patriots" and explained their criminal actions as "the things and events that happen when a sacred landslide victory is so unceremoniously and viciously stripped away from great patriots who have been badly and unfairly treated for so long. Go home in love and peace. Remember this day forever!"[1]

Nothing he said was true. He lost the election. Decisively. In recent speeches, Trump has indicated if he's reelected he will pardon the people serving prison sentences for their criminal actions on January 6.

Mere Prequel

As I sat glued to TV news that fateful day, I felt the wheels could come off the vehicle of democracy. I confess that on January 6, with a moody president oscillating between doing nothing and blaming the whole sordid affair on Speaker of the House Nancy Pelosi, I thought democracy had crashed and burned.

Then I realized January 6 was mere prequel to the next two years. The prequel, which we should have seen coming, has been explained by historian David Blight: "Yet Trumpism unleashed on January 6, and every day before and since over a five-year period, a crusade to slowly poison the American democratic experiment with a movement to overturn

1. Naylor, "Trump's Jan. 6 Speech."

decades of pluralism, increased racial and gender equality, and scientific knowledge. To what end? Establishing a hopeless white utopia for the rich and the aggrieved."[2]

My reasons for writing about Trump are many. Trump is still a danger, a menace to democracy.

"I think our democracy is in trouble," US District Judge Reggie Walton said, "because, unfortunately, we have charlatans like our former president who doesn't, in my view, really care about democracy and only about power."[3]

I Am a Dissident

Most of all, I write because I am a dissident, a dissident in the description offered by Vaclav Havel: "You do not become a 'dissident' just because you decide one day to take up this most unusual career. You are thrown into it by your personal sense of responsibility, combined with a complex set of external circumstances. You are cast out of the existing structures and placed in a position of conflict with them. It begins as an attempt to do your work well and ends with being branded an enemy of society."[4]

Trump represents a movement that has successfully labeled Democrats, liberals, and progressive Christians as the enemy—diabolical, demonic enemies. As a progressive, I am compelled to respond that I am not an enemy of democracy, that I'm neither demon nor devil, but I am a dissident. A dissident may be defined as a person who has decided to live within the truth instead of the toxic environment of lies and religious bigotry that prop up the "Age of Trump."

My overall goal is to show the politics of Trump to be aligned with the ancient politics of the world identified by Saint Paul as that of the "ruler . . . the cosmic powers of this present darkness . . . the spiritual forces of evil."[5]

Of course, this is the opposite of the evangelical insistence that Trump is God's chosen and "anointed one." Trump is neither anointed nor chosen. He stands in the line of an infamous parade that extends from Pharaoh through Pilate, Herod, Caesar, Hitler, Putin, and an assortment

2. Blight, "'Lost Cause' Myth."
3. Mallin, "Judge Slams Trump."
4. Havel, *Power of the Powerless*, 58.
5. Eph 6:12.

of dictators and fascists. He is a cipher on the political stage. If you have seen one Donald Trump, you have seen them all.

I am a dissident, but that is not my profession. A dissident might be considered a person whose profession is grumbling about the state of things. In fact, as a dissident I am simply a Baptist pastor. My dissent is of the order of doing what I feel I must, and this puts me in the crosshairs of many Evangelicals and many Republicans. Being a dissident is my existential attitude.

For seven years, Trump has been undermining democracy with a rhetoric of demolition and dissension. This is a battle between good and evil in a democracy confused about the meaning of good and evil.

A Lesson from Churchill

As Winston Churchill said of Hitler, "This is only the first sip, the first foretaste of a bitter cup which will be preferred to us year by year unless by a supreme recovery of moral health and martial vigor, we arise again and take our stand for freedom as in the olden time."[6]

I am convinced Donald Trump is an evil person on the order of, at least rhetorically, Hitler and intent on the destruction of democracy. I am no Winston Churchill, and I'm not saying Trump *is* Adolf Hitler, but I am drawing comparisons to the rhetoric of Churchill in opposition to Hitler.

Churchill was criticized, castigated, ignored, and considered out of his mind as he consistently warned against the growing power of Hitler. On a lesser scale, perhaps, I assume the same rhetorical stance as Churchill. I believe the warnings about the dangers of Trump are not only necessary for our future safety but are required by all the standards of truth-telling and honesty in our nation.

While the rest of the world ignored Churchill's prophetic warnings, they seemed to be like the people Søren Kierkegaard wrote about in relation to the Bible: "There is always something one has to look into first of all, and it always seems to know one has first of all to have the doctrine in perfect form before one can begin to live—that is say, one never begins."[7]

Perhaps the sense that we should stop talking about Trump allows Trump to continue his demolition of democracy. People say he's just being Donald. People say he means well, but he's just telling it like it is. Even

6. Churchill, "Munich Agreement."

7. Kierkegaard, *Journal of Kierkegaard*, 150.

when his supporters know he is lying, they seem impressed that he can lie and get away with it and not have his political career destroyed.

I don't find any of those excuses plausible. In the epigraph of Timothy Snyder's book *On Tyranny*, there's a memorable quote: "In politics, being deceived is no excuse,"[8] attributed to Leszek Kołakowski.

Churchill said, "I have been mocked and censured as a scaremonger and even a warmonger, by those whose complacency and inertia have brought us all nearer to war and war nearer to us all. But I have the comfort of knowing I have spoken the truth and done my duty. Indeed, I am more proud of the long series of speeches which I have made on defense and foreign policy in the last four years than of anything I have ever been able to do, in all my 40 years of public life."[9]

Donald Trump and his evangelical allies are orchestrating a dark plot to control our government in fundamentalist ways that look like the book of Leviticus overlaid on our Constitution. This is a matter of evil and good that requires diligence and criticism for as long as it takes for this scourge to exhaust itself.

8. Snyder, *On Tyranny*, epigraph.
9. McMenamin, "Action This Day."

Don't Believe Trump's Claims He Will Be "Great for Women and Their Reproductive Rights"

DONALD TRUMP'S CONTROVERSIAL CLAIM on his Truth Social platform that he will be "great for women and their reproductive rights"[1] doesn't break any new ground. All it does is raise suspicions: "Here he goes lying again."

And this is not the first time Trump has claimed he will be "the greatest president" for any number of groups for which he turned out not be the greatest at all: Black people, the LGBTQ community, the middle class.

In reality, the Republican Party is not a leader on in vitro fertilization but is torn between those who support it and those who consider it to be a form of abortion. It was Republican judges in Alabama who made that dreadful ruling against IVF that launched our current national conversation.

Trump sounds like a man whose wife has caught him red-handed in a lie, and he's stammering, "That's my story, and I'm sticking to it."

Politically, will Trump's claim allow him to reclaim women who were switching their votes from Trump to Harris?

Allie Beth Stuckey queried, "How can I still vote for Trump as a Christian after the New York City rally? Easy. I find the unbridled celebration of baby murder seen at Harris rallies as far more vulgar than

---

1. Trump, "I will be great for women."

44

off-color jokes about Puerto Rico."[2] Progressive pastor Zach W. Lambert responded, "The 'unborn' are a convenient group of people to advocate for. They never make demands of you. They are morally uncomplicated, unlike the incarcerated, addicted, or the chronically poor. They don't resent your condescension or complain that you are not politically correct."[3] They still vote for Trump because Harris is considered that bigger devil.

Conservative writer Nancy French, in a Facebook post, offered a positive possibility: "Dear Pro-Lifers who are overlooking Donald Trump's sex abuse conviction, his insurrection, and—well, all of it—because you are pro-life. Your candidate is not. You don't have to do this. You can vote for the Democrat in order to save the GOP and attempt to bring it back to being pro-life!"[4]

Yet former Vice President Mike Pence called Trump's abortion stance a "slap in the face to the millions of pro-life Americans who voted for him in 2016 and 2020."[5]

I applaud the efforts to stop Trump from winning, but I lack confidence the needle will move in "MAGA Land." Trump's system has been in place for nine years, and his supporters ignore all outside criticism. They were not fazed when he lost the hush-money trial. They were not bothered by his conviction on thirty-four felony counts. A popular yard sign in Louisiana read:, "I'm voting for the Felon: Donald Trump."

Trump's Obsession with Being the Greatest

Trump has an addiction to exaggerated claims. Maybe he wants to be P. T. Barnum, architect of "the greatest show on earth." Trump claims to have produced the greatest show on television with his signature call line, "You're fired!"

Using a slogan stolen from President Ronald Reagan, Trump has promised to "Make America Great Again." This promise is itself a lie hiding behind an implied racism and sexism.

When Trump announced his first run for the presidency, reporters thought he went overboard in bragging, "I will be the greatest jobs

2. Stuckey, "How can I still vote."

3. Zach Lambert (@ZachWLambert), "'Unborn' are a convenient group," Oct. 28, 2024, comment on Stuckey, "How can I still vote."

4. French, "Dear Pro-Lifers."

5. Fortinsky, "Trump's Abortion Stance."

president that God has ever created."[6] This claim now sounds hollow since President Bill Clinton, in his speech at the Democratic Convention on August 21, announced that since 1989, Democratic presidents had created fifty million new jobs and Republican presidents only one million. Clinton's claim was independently fact checked and found to be true.[7]

Trump says his crowds are the greatest crowds in the world. When announcing his candidacy for president, Trump said, "It's great to be at Trump Tower. It's great to be in a wonderful city, New York. This has been beyond anybody's expectations. There's been no crowd like this."[8] In reality, actors were paid to attend and wear Trump T-shirts that day.[9]

Shortly after his inauguration, Trump started a lie about his inauguration crowd being larger than Barack Obama's. Yet the video evidence clearly shows Trump's inauguration crowd was smaller than Obama's.

On another fateful day, January 6, 2021, Trump claimed the crowd at his rally that preceded the attack on the US Capitol was in the hundreds of thousands. "The House select committee that investigated the events of Jan. 6, 2021, estimated 53,000 people attended President Donald Trump's speech at the White House Ellipse."[10]

During a news conference at Mar-a-Lago on August 8, 2024, Trump claimed the crowd at his January 6 insurrection speech was larger than the number of people who gathered for the Martin Luther King Jr. "I Have a Dream" speech during the March on Washington for Jobs and Freedom on August 28, 1963. As previously noted, Trump's crowd was estimated at ten thousand; King's crowd, according to the National Archives, two hundred and fifty thousand.[11]

Same Old Trump Song

Trump often has claimed he would be the greatest president for women, for African Americans, and for gays.

---

6. McKay, "15 Head-Scratching Quotes."

7. Rascouët-Paz, "Bill Clinton."

8. Trump, "Presidential Campaign Announcement."

9. Carusone, "Trump Hired Paid Actors"; Couch and McDermott, "Trump Campaign Offered Actors."

10. Jacobson et al., "Trump's False Crowd."

11. Jacobson et al., "Trump's False Crowd."

For example, Trump insisted he's done more for Black Americans than any president since Lincoln: "My Admin has done more for the Black Community than any President since Abraham Lincoln."[12] On June 2, 2020, he tweeted, "My administration is delivering for African Americans like never before. No President has done more for our black community."[13]

Trump's historical vacuity ignores Lincoln's Emancipation Proclamation, the freeing of the slaves. He seems to know nothing of the Thirteenth, Fourteenth, and Fifteenth Amendments passed during President Andrew Johnson's term. And Lyndon Baines Johnson passed the Civil Rights Act. University of Texas history professor H. W. Brands argues that LBJ's Civil Rights Act and Voting Rights Act rank right next to Lincoln's Emancipation Proclamation. "[Johnson's] accomplishments on behalf of African Americans—the Civil Rights Act, the Voting Rights Act, the Fair Housing Act—were historic," said Brands. "Trump's accomplishments were incidental, side effects of a pro-corporate agenda," Brands said.[14]

I lack the space in the article to chronicle all the lies Trump has told around his claim to be the greatest president for women, African Americans, and gays. As representative of all the groups Trump has attempted to lasso into his orbit, I concentrate on his claim he is the best choice for women.

The Art of the Deal: The Trump Strategy

We don't have to make haphazard guesses as to the rhetorical strategy of Donald Trump. He told everyone exactly what he was like in his ghost-written book, *The Art of the Deal*. Trump explains why he talks the way he does. "I play to people's fantasies. . . . People want to believe something is the biggest and the most spectacular. I call it truthful hyperbole. It's an innocent form of exaggeration—and a very effective form of promotion."[15]

Trump's pattern of deception continues uninterrupted in the 2024 presidential campaign. Among his more outrageous lies, Trump openly declares the 2020 election was stolen from him (it wasn't). He lies about crimes committed by illegal immigrants (not much in reality). And he

12. Chalfant, "Trump Claims."
13. Chalfant, "Trump Claims."
14. Jacobson, "Trump Said He's Done More."
15. Skinnell, "What Passes for Truth," 115.

lies about Kamala Harris not being eligible to be a presidential candidate (a new version of the birther conspiracy).

His political career is a Tower of Babel constructed of a scaffolding of lies. The foundation of Trump's "Tower of Lies" is birtherism. He inaugurated his campaign by casting himself as the defender of white maidenhood against Mexican "rapists." A perverse sexual tinge like *50 Shades of Grey* always colors Trump's rhetoric.

Trump's Rap Sheet

Considering the sexualized rhetoric of Trump, we have a record of perverseness unrivaled in American politics. Of the #MeToo movement, Trump said, perhaps naively mirroring his own defense in court, "You've got to deny, deny, deny and push back on these women. If you admit to anything and any culpability, then you're dead. . . . You've got to be strong. You've got to be aggressive. You've got to push back hard. You've got to deny anything that's said about you. Never admit."[16]

Trump claimed *New York Times* columnist Gail Collins had "the face of a dog."[17] He called Stormy Daniels "horseface."[18] Carly Fiorina seemed to scare Trump: "Look at that face. Would anybody vote for that? Can you imagine that, the face of our next president?"[19]

Trump has a proclivity for talking in public about women's looks and bodies. He told French First Lady Brigitte Macron, "You know, you're in such good shape. Beautiful."[20] Maybe even the French were put off by that bit of diplomatic "foot in mouth."

And there's this gem: "Sadly, Heidi Klum is no longer a 10."[21] Asked if Kim Kardashian's butt is big, Trump said, "Well, absolutely. It's record-setting. In the old days, they'd say she has a bad body."[22]

---

16. Oppenheim, "Deny, Deny, Deny."
17. McAdams, "Mind of Donald Trump."
18. Edelman, "Stormy Daniels."
19. Uchimiya, "Trump Insults."
20. Mindock, "Macron's Wife Brigitte."
21. Bueno, "Heidi Klum."
22. Miller, "Revisit."

He made the same kind of male-prejudiced statement about Arianna Huffington: "Unattractive both inside and out. I fully understand why her former husband left her for a man—he made a good decision."[23]

Never shy about speaking of the dead, three weeks after her death, Trump was asked if he could have "nailed" Princess Diana. He responded, "I think I could have."[24] In a 1997 radio interview with Howard Stern just months after Princess Diana's death, Donald Trump insisted that he "could have" had sex with the late British royal—but only would have done so if she passed an HIV test first.

Trump's uncanny wariness of women shows up in his thoughts. He claims women are worse than men and suggests they are real killers.

"Women have one of the great acts of all time," he also said. "The smart ones act very feminine and needy, but inside they are real killers. The person who came up with the expression 'the weaker sex' was either very naive or had to be kidding. I have seen women manipulate men with just a twitch of their eye—or perhaps another body part."[25]

In a statement like his promise to protect reproductive rights, Trump said, "Nobody has more respect for women than I do. Nobody. Nobody has more respect." And this: "I saved your suburbs—women, suburban women, you're supposed to love Trump!"[26]

Like any insecure male, Trump attempts to shore up his ego by attacking women. His gender outrage undergirds his populism and strengthens it. His ostentatious masculine posturing looks like a peacock spreading its plumage. Beneath the surface of his attempt to play nice with women, you can smell his gender outrage.

Trump's machismo combines a deeper bullying, masculine set of performances with a paternalistic dominance. He rejects those whose masculinity he impugns, either by emasculating them or by showing them in a hypermasculine light.

Trump the Rhetorical Pervert

Only one conclusion fits the moral unfitness of Trump's glaring sexism, disrespect, dishonesty, and bad behavior: pervert.

23. Heller, "Arianna Huffington."
24. McAfee, "Donald Trump Once Boasted."
25. Bahadur, "22 Sexist Things."
26. Reston, "Trump Continues Bizarre Appeals."

As Joshua Gunn notes in *Political Perversion*, even with Trump's repeated statements that tempt the most widespread cultural taboo there is ("If Ivanka weren't my daughter, perhaps I'd be dating her"), very few critics reference the former president as a "pervert."[27]

Trump is not promising to protect women's reproductive rights; he is "Trumpeteering" for votes under any possible pretense. To listen to Trump promise to keep women safe is like inviting a sexual offender into your living room when you are alone.

The truth is Trump is incapable of being the greatest president for women because he has no respect for women. The pattern of his despicable treatment of women is as long as his support of birtherism. He is afraid of women. He has no idea how to deal with Kamala Harris. So far, he has attacked her for being stupid and for allegedly being a communist. He will need to do better.

Trump is not a friend of women. He is not a protector of women. And there's no way he will be "great for women and their reproductive rights."

---

27. Gunn, *Political Perversion*, 117.

There's a Crazy Index for Donald Trump

I S IT JUST ME or is Donald Trump getting crazier by the day?
How is it possible for a man who is a congenital liar, a convicted felon, a con man, and a fraud who happens to be emotionally
and mentally unstable to still be in a tight race for the presidency? Crazy
as it sounds, "Crazy" is one heartbeat from the White House—again.

There's no questioning whether Trump's rallies are getting weirder.
One of his followers physically attacked a member of the press at the
Johnstown, Pennsylvania, rally on August 31. Video of the incident
shows Trump actively encouraging the man as he was being tackled by
security. Trump called the attack "beautiful." Then he said, "That's alright.
That's OK. No, he's on our side."[1]

Trump and his Magadonians actively encouraging and cheering a
fellow supporter for an act of violence certainly registers as crazy. I would
like to imagine Trump's new penchant for saying the craziest possible
things will finally flip the switch and cause some of his supporters to desert him. Or failing to lose a single Magadonian, perhaps people thinking
about voting for Trump will change their minds and say, "He's crazy." I
am not convinced it will make much difference, but I am determined to
make a gargantuan effort.

I have devised (with a helping hand from something known as The
Rapture Index) what I label The Crazy Index.

---

1. Walker, "Trump Tells Supporters."

The Crazy Index

The Crazy Index attempts to keep track of the number of crazy statements made by Donald Trump. These remarks are factored into a cohesive indicator. The Crazy Index is designed to measure the increasing danger posed by Trump descending into crazier and crazier rhetoric.

The Crazy Index is the Dow Jones Industrial Average of crazy statements, indicating the diminished mental acuity of Trump.

The Crazy Index currently has thirty-five categories of crazy comments made by Trump recently. Each category receives a numerical value of one to five. The crazier the statement, the higher the number the category receives.

If Trump made crazy statements in all thirty-five categories and each statement rated a score of five, The Crazy Meter Score for Trump would be 175. All politicians engage in less-than-truthful comments, hyperbole, or stretch the truth with stories. The average among American politics is 20 percent. That would be a score of 35.

The higher the number, the faster we're moving toward the Republican nominee for president being too crazy to be our president.

"I'll Take a Baker's Dozen of Crazy"

Immigration

"Why is it that millions of people were allowed to come into our country from prisons, from jails, from mental institutions, insane asylums, even insane asylums, that's a—it's a mental institution on steroids. That's what it is."[2]

Previously Trump referred to immigrants as "poisoning the blood" of real Americans. No one missed the Nazi language. In case someone missed the connection, Hitler provided a "symbolic rebirth," and "a symbolic change of lineage" from the "Hebrew prophets" as the "spiritual ancestors of Christianity." In doing so, "he renounces this 'ancestry' in a 'materialistic' way by voting himself and the members of his lodge a different 'blood stream' from that of the Jews."[3]

This is crazy because on the day he announced his run for the presidency, Trump already was crazy: "When Mexico sends its people,

2. Montanaro, "Lies and Distortions."
3. Burke, "Rhetoric of Hitler's 'Battle,'" 203.

they're not sending their best. . . . They're sending people that have lots of problems and they're bringing those problems with us. They're bringing drugs. They're bringing crime. They're rapists."[4]

Magnets

At a rally in Iowa, Trump went off on a strange tale about magnets. "Think of it, magnets," he said. "Now all I know about magnets is this, give me a glass of water, let me drop it on the magnets, that's the end of the magnets. Why didn't they use John Deere? Why didn't they bring in the John Deere people? Do you like John Deere? I like John Deere."[5]

Ron Filipkowski, editor-in-chief for Meidas Touch, said, "Dementia Trump is riffing on his magnets in a water story, then tries to pander to the Iowa audience by bringing John Deere into the story because what's in his head to repeat in IA over and over is 'John Deere,' and the whole deal just short circuits into an addled, sweaty mess."[6]

Kamala Harris

Trump used his social media website to amplify a crude remark about Vice President Kamala Harris that suggested she traded sexual favors to help her political career. The post, by another user on Truth Social, was an image of Harris and Hillary Clinton, Trump's opponent in 2016. The text read, "Funny how blowjobs impacted both their careers differently."[7]

The remark was a reference to Clinton's husband, former President Bill Clinton, and the Monica Lewinsky scandal, and an unfounded right-wing contention that Harris's once-upon-a-time romantic relationship with Willie Brown, the former mayor of San Francisco whom she dated in the mid-1990s while he was speaker of the California State Assembly, fueled her political rise.

Trump's response to his own vulgarity and lack of decency will be his favorite defense: "I didn't say it. I simply reposted it."[8]

4. McKay, "15 Head-Scratching Quotes."
5. Kika, "Donald Trump Ridiculed."
6. Filipkowski, "Dementia Trump."
7. Nieto, "Shockingly Crass Comment."
8. Mercieca, *Demagogue for President*, 127.

Hannibal Lecter

Trump has compared migrants to the character Hannibal Lecter in the film *The Silence of the Lambs*. He says of immigrants, "They're rough people, in many cases from jails, prisons, from mental institutions, insane asylums," he said of migrants who enter the country unlawfully. "You know, insane asylums, that's 'Silence of the Lambs' stuff." In the 1991 movie, Hannibal Lecter is a serial killer and a cannibal.

"Hannibal Lecter, anybody know Hannibal Lecter?" he added to audience laughter at his Mar-a-Lago estate in Palm Beach, Florida. "We don't want 'em in this country."

"Silence of the lambs! The late great Hannibal Lecter. It is a wonderful man."[9] Trump repeatedly has said Hannibal Lecter, a fictional serial killer, is a "great man" who deserves our "congratulations"—so why keep him out of the US?

He seems confused about whether Hannibal Lecter is a character or the man who played him in a movie. He's remarked, "Hannibal Lecter, how great an actor was he?" Trump has said he loves Lecter because the actor once said, "I love Donald Trump" in a TV interview.

By the end of *The Silence of the Lambs*, Lecter has escaped from the Baltimore State Hospital for the Criminally Insane and is stalking his next victim in the Bahamas. Yet Trump just loves yelling "Hannibal Lecter!" at his rallies, even if it is crazy.

Robert E. Lee, Gettysburg, and the Pirate Jack Sparrow

In an April rally, after describing the Battle of Gettysburg, in which about fifty thousand soldiers died—in Trump's words, "So beautiful in so many different ways"—he delivered a fake quote from Confederate General Robert E. Lee in a bad Captain Jack Sparrow voice: "Robert E. Lee, who's no longer in favor—did you ever notice it? He's no longer in favor. 'Never fight uphill, me boys, never fight uphill.' They were fighting uphill. He said, 'Wow, that was a big mistake.' He lost his great general. . . . 'Never fight uphill, me boys!' But it was too late."[10]

9. All quotes concerning Hannibal Lecter from Lebowitz and Traylor, "Hannibal Lecter."

10. Mazza, "'Dimbulb' Trump."

Tim Walz

"His nickname is Tampon," Trump told an audience full of National Guard members, many of whom wore their camouflage uniforms. "Tampon Tim Walz,"[11] he said later, alluding to a Minnesota bill that Walz, as governor, helped pass requiring access to menstrual products in public schools.

I think Trump has been reading old Putin speeches. Putin once defended the Motherland (Russia) as a "man's affair," telling women he did not need to engage in public debates on which was better, "Tampax or Snickers."[12]

Inflation

If he were still president, "there would be no inflation," Trump claims. "A lot of great things would have happened, but now you have millions and millions of dead people. And you have people dying financially, because they can't buy bacon; they can't buy food; they can't buy groceries; they can't do anything. And they're living horribly in our country right now."[13]

Among other things, Trump is lying about the price of bacon. Maybe it is because Kamala Harris could have starred in that television ad from the 1990s. The woman says, "I can bring up the bacon, fry it up in the pan, and still make you feel like a man." Trump doesn't have a clue what to do about strong, intelligent women. And his understanding of the American economy is crazy.

Abortion

"I think the abortion issue has been very much tempered down, and I've answered I think very well in the debate, and it seems to be much less of an issue, especially for those where they have the exceptions," Trump said. "As you know, and I think it's when I look for 52 years, they wanted to bring abortion back to the states. They wanted to get rid of Roe v. Wade and

---

11. Folk, "Truth Social Insult Spree."
12. Eksi and Wood, "Right-Wing Populism," 740.
13. Page, "Trump Bizarrely Claims."

that's Democrats, Republicans and Independents and everybody. Liberals, conservatives, everybody wanted it back in the states. And I did that."[14]

In addition to saying all Democrats wanted Roe v. Wade overturned, Trump continues to accuse Democrats of killing babies after they are born. Trump posted, "Senate Democrats just voted against legislation to prevent the killing of newborn infant children. The Democratic position on abortion is now so extreme that they don't mind executing babies after birth."[15]

"Actively killing an infant born alive is a crime," said Lois Shepherd, a professor of law and biomedical ethics at the University of Virginia and author of the books *Rationing Health Care at the End of Life* and *If That Ever Happens to Me: Making Life and Death Decisions After Terri Schiavo*. "Under the law, living infants are just like other living people. They are children. Children are people."[16]

Trump also declared his administration would be "great for women and their reproductive rights."

He has been pro-choice and anti-abortion. He has bragged about getting rid of *Roe* and now wants to be for reproductive rights. He is a high-speed yo-yo on a string. He's doing loops and tricks.

An Outlandish Array of Claims

The Assassination Attempt

"I think to a certain extent it's Biden's fault and Harris' fault," he said of the attempted assassination against him on July 13, 2024.[17]

Election Denial and Indictment

On Fox News, Trump offered what sounded like a confession: "Whoever heard you get indicted for interfering with a presidential election, where you have every right to do it, you get indicted, and your poll numbers go up."[18]

14. Ibssa and Kim, "Trump Boasts of Role."
15. Trump, "Senate Democrats just voted."
16. Jacobson, "Fact-Checking."
17. Price and Weissert, "Trump Blames."
18. Jane, "Cognitive Decline?"

Putting On His Pants

"First they say, 'Sir, how do you do it? How do you wake up in the morning and put on your pants?'" Trump mused. "And I say, 'Well, I don't think about it too much.' I don't want to think about it because if I think about it too much maybe I won't want to do it, but I love it because we're going to do something for this country that's never been done before."[19]

Digital Trading Cards

Nothing says "crazy" like the former president marketing digital trading cards for ninety-nine dollars each in an effort to raise cash. The images of Trump on the cards make him Superman. The man who would be president has side hustles selling gold athletic shoes (the Wicked Witch of the West would be envious), Bibles, and trading cards. The digital trading cards are the clearest evidence of a man who has gone down the rabbit hole.

Women as Voters

While his polling with women falters, Trump praised his supporters' husbands for "allowing" their wives to attend his campaign rallies without them. "Somebody said, 'Women don't like Donald Trump,'" he said in Johnstown, Pennsylvania, August 30. "I said, 'I think that's wrong. I think they love me.' I love them."[20]

He pointed to a group of women from North Carolina who have attended 227 of his rallies: "They're wealthy as hell. Look at them. They've got nothing but cash. Their husbands are great. But they allow them to go all over the country."

He recalled a conversation with some of their husbands where he asked, "How do you put up with this? Your wives are traveling all over the place. Do you mind?"

The husbands told him, "'We trust our wives, sir. We trust them implicitly.'"

Trump's response was to say the women are "always perfectly coiffed. . . . They're beautiful."

19. Jane, "Cognitive Decline?"
20. Quotes in this section come from Trump, "Johnstown, PA."

A Box of Doughnut Holes to Go
with Your Baker's Dozen

That baker's dozen alone blows the top out of the Crazy Index, but there's more, so much more.

There are his crazy statements about interest rates, the economy, oil prices, climate change, the stock market, leadership, Israel, Ukraine, guns, liberalism, how crazy Kamala Harris is, crime rates, civil rights, the food supply, gangs, a nation in decline, the border, sharks, and Nazis.

My fear is that as lying hasn't hurt Trump, he will still be the MAGA sweetheart when he has "gone around the bend"—if he hasn't already.

Yes, I want Trump's Achilles's heel to be his own crazy words. As he descends into illusion, excess hyperbole, deep-rooted demaguery, and self-praise, as he says crazier and crazier stuff, I want to see his poll numbers drop into Dante's last hell. By my math, Trump's Crazy Index Score already is 165. He's crazy.

Instead of profanity, a strong push for rational thought, deliberation, and debate should return to the center of our politics. As long as Trump keeps saying stuff like this at his rallies and on Truth Social, and as long as his defenders—including J. D. Vance—keep showing up on national news shows to defend his insane statements, we will remain stuck in the crazy cycle. And that's exactly where Trump wants the nation to be.

He insists he isn't incoherent; he's just misunderstood. "The fake news will say 'Trump is rambling,'" he declared recently in Philadelphia. "No, it's genius what I'm doing up here, but nobody understands."[21]

There it is in a nutshell: We say, "Crazy." Trump says, "I'm a genius."

21. Trump, "Rally in Philadelphia."

Trump's Plan to Fight Anti-Semitism Is More Authoritarianism

I T IS A DOCUMENTED fact that anti-Semitism is on the rise not only in the United States but globally. Donald Trump has a plan to fight this: deport university students.

Amid the flurry of executive orders flying out of the Oval Office since January 20, Trump signed one on anti-Semitism. He appears to address the campus protests that happened nearly two years ago in reaction to Israeli Prime Minister Benjamin Netanyahu waging war on Palestinians in Gaza.

Before getting to his latest actions, Trump referred back to his first term in office when on December 11, 2019, he issued another executive order "finding that students, in particular, faced antisemitic harassment in schools and on university and college campuses."[1]

That was four years before the surprise Hamas attack on Israel that prompted Netanyahu's revenge, which sparked campus protests nationwide.

Now back in office, Trump has picked up the theme from 2019: "Immediate action will be taken by the Department of Justice to protect law and order, quell pro-Hamas vandalism and intimidation, and investigate and punish anti-Jewish racism in leftist, anti-American colleges and universities. To all the resident aliens who joined in the pro-jihadist protests, we put you on notice: Come 2025, we will find you, and we will deport you. I will also quickly cancel the student visas of all Hamas sympathizers

---

1. Exec. Order No. 14188, Fed. Reg. 2025-02230, §1.

on college campuses, which have been infested with radicalism like never before."[2]

Trump's plan to fight anti-Semitism is to use the powers of the federal government to go after universities and to deport people, including students, who are here on visas if the protests in which they are participating are deemed to be sympathetic to Hamas.

Let's be clear: College students protesting what they saw in Israel's invasion of Gaza is not anti-Semitism. Opposing the military policy of Netanyahu is not an act of anti-Semitism.

Even Israelis have taken to the streets of Tel Aviv and Jerusalem to protest Netanyahu's war.

Is there an upsurge of anti-Semitism in the United States? Yes. Does it require an executive order aimed only at colleges? No.

Bundled Racism

Trump's executive order is part of a bundle that has to do with far more than anti-Semitism. It has to do with anti-democracy.

Look at his other executive orders and proclamations about "school choice" programs and defunding schools teaching Critical Race Theory or gender issues. Look at the announcement from the Department of Defense that it will no longer celebrate cultural awareness months, including Black History Month.

As BNG previously reported, Trump and his allies consistently define anti-Semitism in a way that lets them off the hook for their own biases.

Speech professor Ira J. Allen notes, "Racialized hatred of all sorts are consubstantial with one another and with Trumpism. Antisemitism flies in the same constellation of other forms of racialized hate belonging to Trump's vision to 'Make America Great Again.' The misogyny, the racism, the transphobia, the antisemitism and the nativism are all part of the same Trump bundle."[3]

Trump seamlessly blends patriotism, nationalism, racism, and anti-Semitism into one package. There's a straight line from deporting "terrorist" students to deporting eleven million immigrants—the Trump ethnic cleansing pogrom.

2. The White House, "Combat Anti-Semitism."
3. Allen, "Donald Trump's Antisemitism," 67.

What Is Anti-Semitism?

Since the president insists on the ruse of "anti-Semitism," a solid understanding of exactly what is meant by the term is required. According to the Merriam-Webster dictionary, anti-Semitism means hostility to or prejudice against Jewish people.[4]

The US Department of State defines "anti-Semitism" according to the Stockholm Declaration and the IHRA Plenary in Bucharest: "Antisemitism is a certain perception of Jews, which may be expressed as hatred toward Jews. Rhetorical and physical manifestations of antisemitism are directed toward Jewish or non-Jewish individuals and/or their property, toward Jewish community institutions and religious facilities."[5]

Most Americans are not, according to these definitions, anti-Semitic. There are, of course, anti-Semitic groups in America. The Southern Poverty Law Center lists thirty-one neo-Nazi groups in the US. Neo-Nazi groups share a hatred for Jews and a love for Adolf Hitler and Nazi Germany.

An ABC News / *Washington Post* poll found one in ten Americans think it's "acceptable" to hold neo-Nazi views. (In contrast, 83 percent say it's unacceptable, and 8 percent had no opinion on neo-Nazism.[6]) These numbers suggest due diligence in resisting anti-Semitism but not a cause for too much alarm.

How Can You Say Trump Is an Anti-Semite?

Why should we bother with saying Trump is anti-Semitic? He denies it: "I'm the least antisemitic person you've ever seen in your entire life."[7] This parallels his "least racist person" and "I love women and women love me" insincere remarks.

Trump's son-in-law Jared Kushner is a Jew and a member of Chabad. His grandchildren are Jewish. His daughter converted to Judaism in 2009. Trump is a huge supporter of Israel. He moved the American embassy to Jerusalem. He appointed Mike Huckabee as US ambassador

---

4. Merriam-Webster, s.v. "anti-Semitism."
5. International Holocaust Remembrance Alliance, "Antisemitism."
6. ABC News, "Neo-Nazi Views."
7. Watkins, "Sit Down."

to Israel. The same Mike Huckabee who has said, "There's really no such thing as a Palestinian."[8]

Here's the dilemma. If Trump is as personally close to Judaism and as politically close to Israel as any American president has ever been, why is his own political rise coupled with the rise of anti-Semitism and celebrated by anti-Semites?

When Trump was first elected in 2016, there was a dramatic surge in incidences of anti-Semitism. The Anti-Defamation League reported an 86 percent increase in anti-Semitic incidents in the first quarter of 2017. Through the first nine months of 2017, there were 1,299 incidents of anti-Semitic assault, harassment, or vandalism. During this time period, 160 synagogues received bomb threats, and Jewish cemeteries were vandalized across the country.[9] Anti-Semitism and racism have stuck to Trump since his earliest days in business.

This is revelatory: anti-Semitism isn't rising from college students protesting but from Trump promoting his ideology of white supremacy. Adept at rolling all his prejudices into one statement, Trump once said, "Black guys counting my money! I hate it. The only kind of people I want counting my money are short guys that wear yarmulkes every day."[10]

Anti-Semitism in Trump Administration

If the Trump administration were serious about fighting anti-Semitism, it would stop scapegoating college students and start addressing the rampant anti-Semitic people in its own administration. These Trump surrogates are part of the dodge.

There's Elon Musk. He has given a Nazi-like salute, posted pro-Nazi puns, and spoken to a far-right Nazi party in Germany to get over their guilt and be proud of being Germans. Does Musk know that "Making Germany Great Again" by restoring German racial pride was the primary rhetorical strategy of Hitler?

There's Stephen Miller, author of the family separation policy for immigrants. When a trove of emails were released showing Miller's white nationalist views, Jewish organizations spoke against him. They called

---

8. Kaczynski, "Mike Huckabee."

9. The White House, "Combat Anti-Semitism."

10. Coates, "First White President."

Miller a white nationalist and the architect of the Trump administration's cruel and endless attacks on immigrants.

There's the director of ICE, Tom Homan, who told *60 Minutes* he didn't write the memo for deporting immigrants, he was only following orders. My memory shifted automatically to General Himmler testifying at his war trial he only made sure the trains ran on schedule, and he didn't kill anyone.

Trump's multipiece ideology fits together to make one clear picture: he marks off Jews as "other" just as he marks off Black people, brown people, Muslim people, LGBTQ people, and trans people.

Trump Undermines Human Rights

Trump policies ultimately hurt Jews because they undermine basic human rights. Jews, perhaps more than other people, should know better than to advocate for a disliked minority to lose its rights.

Hugh Taylor, blogger for the *Times of Israel*, argues, "American Jews should remember that anything that can be done for us can also be done to us. It should trouble us that the executive order can target people for deportation based on vague and frighteningly flexible parameters like 'hostile attitudes toward its citizens, culture, government, institutions.'"[11]

Amy Spitalnick, head of the liberal Jewish Council for Public Affairs, said in a statement opposing Trump's executive order, "It is both possible and necessary to directly confront and address the crisis of anti-semitism, on campus and across our communities, without abandoning the fundamental democratic values that have allowed Jews, and so many others, to thrive here."[12]

First Amendment

One executive order at a time, Trump continues his assault on liberal democracy. Perry Bacon Jr. at the *Washington Post* argues this is "a full-scale war against modern liberalism. This executive order, in its attack on institutions of higher learning and on the constitutional right to free assembly and needs to be understood in that context."[13]

11. Taylor, "Should We Celebrate."
12. Spitalnick, "JCPA Responds."
13. Bacon, "Trump's First Moves."

Even more haunting: this is but the first salvo in the coming war against American universities by a right-wing evangelical mob already intoxicated with more than a century of anti-intellectualism rooted in anti-science and anti-history ideologies.

Taylor says in the *Times of Israel*, "Trump is using Jewish fear and the threat of antisemitism to attack civil rights, minorities and democracy itself while allowing antisemitism in his own administration to fester."[14]

Deporting students is not action against anti-Semitism; it is governmental bullying that is grossly antidemocratic.

"The First Amendment protects everyone in the United States, including foreign citizens studying at American universities," said Carrie DeCell, senior staff attorney at the Knight First Amendment Institute at Columbia University. "Deporting non-citizens on the basis of their political speech would be unconstitutional."[15]

All of us need to reject both Trump's anti-Semitism and his authoritarianism. To accomplish this task, we need as many "others" as possible.

14. Taylor, "Should We Celebrate."
15. Granieri, "Trump Proposal."

I Imagine Jesus Saying to Trump, "Not Everyone Posting a Sketch of Me with Them Will Enter the Kingdom of Heaven"

A N ANONYMOUS FAN OF ex-president Donald Trump produced a sketch of Jesus sitting in court with Trump, which Trump then posted on his Truth Social platform.[1]

The closest I can come to understanding this travesty is to admit the desire to have Jesus on our side seems as natural as breathing. There's something about being in trouble and wanting to identify with Jesus.

In this painting of Jesus sitting next to him, Trump reflects the image of an ordinary person in trouble. What is noxious and toxic here is that Trump's followers find his body and face as glorious as Jesus—and a very white Jesus at that.

Jesus sitting in court with Trump as his chief defender resonates with Evangelicals who created Trump as the new "Cyrus"—God's anointed. Perhaps this is a matter of perception. Perhaps if one believes Jesus would be sitting there with Trump, it's easier to believe Trump should be found innocent of the multitude of indictments he faces.

Or maybe what many Trump supporters really care about is that Trump swears he will put America first, stand up for them, be their voice. Maybe that's all that matters.

Or maybe it's even less than that. Maybe what Trump supporters care about is merely that they get to feel good about being on Jesus' side.

1. Neath, "Bizarre Court Sketch."

And if they are on Jesus' side, then it is only logical to assume Jesus will be there with Trump in court.

Trump followers do not care about his lying. They are not put off by his convictions, his indictments, his toxic, degrading rhetoric—because they like it. They don't really care about Jesus. Jesus is in the picture as a prop—a religious artifact like the bones of a prophet or the Shroud of Turin. Nothing matters except the image.

Jesus props up all the lies, fantasies, and illusions of Trump and his clan.

Trump's Face Speaks the Truth

Instead of gazing at the superficial, tacky picture of the guy alleged to be Jesus, look at the face of Trump. Trump's face, I would suggest, is a major component of his self-image, one his followers have embraced.

Paul Achter points out, "He is extremely self-conscious about how he is represented in the media. He reads and watches stories about himself, sending journalists feedback, calling TV shows, and always trying to influence coverage. His staff delivers screenshots of his TV coverage to him after major events so he can see how he looks and what chyrons are paired with what images. Although he cannot control the way he is represented, he is more invested than ever in trying."[2]

Thus, Trump had a public relations expert's reason for reposting a courtroom sketch of him with Jesus.

This does not mean the presence of Jesus in the image is irrelevant. It means Jesus' presence only has the meaning Trump wants it to have for his followers. He's reminding them that even sitting in court, facing indictment, in a trial where he already has been found guilty, he is still God's anointed, the messiah of MAGA, the savior of America.

Jesus sits next to Trump because sitting on the judicial bench and in the shadows are the judge and the evil Democrats leading the "witch hunt."

On Trump's face there's no sense of being humble, contrite, or repentant. Instead, he's the usual Trump projected in his images: stern, square-jawed, unsmiling, rigid, dominating, glaring. The eyes stare straight ahead looking everywhere, looking at nothing.

---

2. Achter, "Great Television," 116.

This sketch captures the image Trump projects to the world. Even his official portraits as president show him in the same posture.

In most of his photos—even his booking photo at the county jail in Georgia—there is a slight smirk at the corner of his mouth and a bit of a sneer on his upper lip. What you see is what the media-conscious Trump wants you to see: he is completely in charge; he is the toughest guy in the room. He is a controlling, dominating presence, and no one is ever allowed to forget it.

Even in his now-famous mug shot, the *New York Times'* Maggie Haberman says Trump gave a "menacing" stare because he "doesn't want to look weak."[3] Known as the "Kubrick stare," Trump's look has been used often by actors to depict ultimate derangement.

Trump's stare obliterates shame, guilt, any sense of wrong. Trump supporters admire the glaring, staring, stony images of their hero.

Julian Raven, an upstate New York artist, has created a painting dubbed *Unashamed and Unafraid*, in which Trump's face dominates the foreground.[4] A screeching bald eagle emerges from the horizon, trailing an American flag in its talons. The frigid stare is matched by the glare of the attacking eagle. The artist depicts an aggressive sense of dignity in the face of shame. There's no apology, no repentance in this face.

And that makes the image of Trump and Jesus hard to dissect, even harder to imagine. The two images are exact opposites.

Trump reposted this sketch by an unknown fan, but he seemed unaware of the contradictions. Trump never would appear in a photo where another man has better hair, and this Jesus looks like the star of a Head and Shoulders ad.

On Trial with Jesus

The possible meanings of Trump next to Jesus activates other images. The artist puts Jesus on trial with Trump. I am not sure the artist thought this through because trials have not been good for Jesus and his faithful followers. This image has Jesus sitting next to Trump as if Jesus is on trial as a codefendant. But Jesus is not a codefendant like Rudy Giuliani, Sidney Powell, or Mike Lindell and the sordid bunch of Trump acolytes doing their master's dirty work.

3. Dorman, "Maggie Haberman."
4. Raven, "Trump Painting."

At his trial, Jesus was mocked, scourged, and sentenced to death. In case you missed the image of being next to Jesus at trial, recall the account of Saint Luke:

> Two others also, who were criminals, were led away to be put to death with him. When they came to the place that is called The Skull, they crucified Jesus there with the criminals, one on his right and one on his left. One of the criminals who was hanged there kept deriding him and saying, "Are you not the Messiah? Save yourself and us!" But the other rebuked him, saying, "Do you not fear God, since you are under the same sentence of condemnation? And we indeed have been condemned justly, for we are getting what we deserve for our deeds, but this man has done nothing wrong." Then he said, "Jesus, remember me when you come into your kingdom." He replied, "Truly I tell you, today you will be with me in Paradise."[5]

I'm not sure Trump wants to be sitting next to Jesus at a trial. While Trump isn't facing the death penalty, losing his prized New York businesses will feel like death to him. Trump cares more about Trump Tower and his vast New York holdings than all his other properties combined.

Trump Tower's gleaming orange-and-pink marble and gold interior is the symbol of Donald Trump. He has plastered his name everywhere. All that is now threatened, and the idea of Jesus being with him must appeal to a man who now smells of desperation.

He is a fan of gilding—of adding a thin layer of gold to things to make them appear more valuable than they are. This appears to be how he has valued his real estate when seeking loans—gilding. And that is what Jesus is doing in this latest image, providing the gilding to cover the multitude of his own crimes.

Jennifer Mercieca, a Texas A&M communication professor, says, "Trump has lived his life as a Sun King of sorts—he has believed himself to be above the law, never permitting himself to be held accountable for his actions. In fact, Trump takes pride in his Sun King–like ability to decide what is and what is not. 'The Golden Rule of Negotiating,' Trump once tweeted to his followers, is 'He who has the gold makes the rules.'"[6]

Trump has long presented himself as the messiah of the nation. When he accepted the Republican nomination for president, he incredulously proclaimed, "Every day I wake up determined to deliver for the

5. Luke 23:32–43.
6. Buetler, "Trump's Many Outrages."

people I have met all across this nation that have been neglected, ignored and abandoned. I have visited the laid-off factory workers and the communities crushed by our horrible and unfair trade deals. These are the forgotten men and women of our country. People who work hard but no longer have a voice. I AM YOUR VOICE!"[7]

Trump said "I alone can fix it. I will restore law and order." Yoni Appelbaum observed, "He did not appeal to prayer, or to God. He did not ask Americans to measure him against their values, or to hold him responsible for living up to them. He did not ask for their help. He asked them to place their faith in him."[8]

More Idolatry

When you have an ex-president of the United States reposting a courtroom sketch of himself with Jesus, you know you have a problem. The Trinity is not a political illusion of God, Jesus, and Trump. That Trump would project an image of Jesus being on his side and have his supporters going "gaga" over the image is evidence that some Americans no longer know how to recognize idolatry.

Remember the photo op Trump created with him holding a Bible—sometimes upside down—in front of a church across the street from the White House?

And remember that Trump previously attempted to connect his plight to that of President Abraham Lincoln.

Trump attempting to get Jesus on his defense team runs into factual discrepancies. Jesus clearly says, "Turn the other cheek."[9] Trump has suggested the Bible verse he loves is "an eye for an eye and a tooth for a tooth."[10] Jesus did quote the "eye for an eye" text but only to show it didn't meet his requirements for his followers.

Trump attacks his enemies with a fierceness never before seen in American politics. Jesus, while hanging from a cross, said, "Father, forgive them, for they know not what they do."[11]

---

7. Plumer, "Acceptance Speech."

8. Appelbaum, "I Alone Can Fix It."

9. Matt 5:38.

10. Exod 21:24.

11. Luke 23:34.

The more images that are produced with Trump claiming Jesus is on his side, the more obvious it becomes that this is a thinly disguised piece of religious gilding. Among the many paintings of Trump with Jesus, there's one of Jesus standing behind Trump in the Oval Office guiding his hand as he signs an executive order.

There's Jesus and Trump walking on water. Peter must be jealous. He never could quite get the hang of walking on water without sinking to the bottom.

There's Trump standing before a crowd with his arms extended out from his waist, and in the background Jesus hangs from a cross with his arms extended.

That's my conclusion. Trump reposted the courtroom sketch of Jesus sitting next to him because he's "not taking any chances." To paraphrase Jesus, "Not everyone posting a sketch of me with them will enter the kingdom of heaven."

Using Trump's favorite rhetorical trope of paralipsis, "I'm not saying Trump isn't going to heaven, I'm just saying!"

Are Young Voters Switching to Trump over Israel's War?

Y OUNG VOTERS SUPPORTING DONALD Trump over Joe Biden makes me catch my breath. How is it possible that an indicted insurrectionist who lies routinely has such support among young people? Have our young people lost their collective minds?

But yet here is the latest headline. Nate Cohn, chief political analyst for the *New York Times*, asks, "How much is Biden's support of Israel hurting him with young voters?"[1]

Cohn notes that according to a brand-new *New York Times* / Siena College national survey, Trump now leads Joe Biden among young voters 49 percent to 43 percent. Complicating the picture is a dramatic generational gap.[2]

In the current war in the Middle East, voters ages sixty-five and older sympathize with Israel more than Palestinians by a nearly six to one margin. That level of support slowly decreases among each age group until it reaches young Americans. A near majority of registered voters ages eighteen to twenty-nine (46 percent) sympathize more with Palestinians.

This alone represents a stark change in American support for Israel. What remains to be seen is whether young voters also are attracted to the rising anti-Semitism in the United States. It's one thing to criticize the government of Israel, as even many Jews in Israel are doing in daily protests. A darker, more sinister demon arises when the discussion shifts to anti-Semitism.

1. Cohen, "Biden's Support of Israel."
2. Cohen, "Biden's Support of Israel."

Two-thirds (67 percent) of young Americans between the ages of eighteen and twenty-four believe Jews as a class are oppressors and should be treated as oppressors, according to a new poll conducted by Harris Insights and Analytics and Harvard University's Center for American Political Studies. Fifty-one percent of eighteen-to-twenty-four-year-olds believe the long-term answer for the Israeli-Palestinian conflict is for Israel to be ended and given to Hamas and the Palestinians.

Among Americans between the ages of eighteen and twenty-four, some 73 percent also said they think the Hamas attack on Israel was a terrorist attack, and three-fourths (66 percent) said it was genocidal in nature, but 60 percent also said it could be justified by the grievances of Palestinians.[3]

Evidence suggests current support for Trump over Biden may have more to do with frustration than it does with young people believing Trump would help the Palestinians. Trump initially criticized Israeli leadership over the Hamas terrorist attacks on October 7 but since has reiterated his support for the country. He has insisted he would take a much harder line against Iran, which has long backed the military wing of Gaza's governing body, but has suggested the Israel-Hamas conflict will have to play out.

Trump also moved the US embassy in Israel from Tel Aviv to Jerusalem, fulfilling a pledge to evangelical Christians in America who are among the most strident supporters of both the Jewish people and the state of Israel.

The Biden administration's approach to the war has given growing support for humanitarian aid pauses that in part also allow for civilians to leave Gaza for safer places. Trump has said he would reject refugees from Gaza from entering the United States, and he has called for ideological screenings for those entering the country.

The issue for young people, then, does not seem to be a serious consideration of policies. More emotional issues seem to be in play.

According to Jonathan Weisman, Ruth Igielnik, and Alyce McFadden, the anti-Biden surge relates directly to an "extraordinarily negative view of Israel's recent conduct."[4]

Young voters believe Israel is not doing enough to prevent civilian casualties in Gaza. In addition, they don't believe Israel is interested in

3. Center for American Political Studies, "Harvard CAPS Harris Poll."
4. Weisman et al., "Poll Finds."

peace, and they think Israel should end the war in Gaza, even if Hamas is not eliminated.

Opposition to the war itself is probably contributing to Biden's unusual weakness among young voters.

A closer look at the survey of young people shows nonvoters are primarily responsible for the surge in Trump support. This represents a troubling trend. Nonvoters, by not voting, already have indicated a lack of support for democratic values. They are, like church members who never attend church, stuck on a voter roll somewhere but have no meaningful engagement with democratic processes.

For young people to be disgusted by Israel's invasion of Gaza makes sense, but why would this disgust lead to a switch from President Biden to support of the ex-president, Donald Trump?

Support for Trump among nonvoting young people may be the result of the uncanny ability of Trump to use his demagogic skills to entice support. Patricia Roberts-Miller, in her study of demagoguery, demonstrates the demagogue has no interest in advancing democratic deliberation.[5] A demagogue uses rhetorical strategies like scapegoating and oversimplifying complicated situations to take advantage of the uninformed and disengaged.

Trump, more than any candidate in recent American politics, attracts the social media crowd. In *The Twitter Presidency*, Brian L. Ott and Greg Dickinson argue that Trump is effective as a communicator precisely by virtue of his ability to ignite a latent fund of frustration. In addition, they suggest Twitter is a uniquely effective tool for Trump by virtue of its medium-specific affordances in favor of simplicity, impulsivity, and incivility.[6]

Trump's ability to garner support from the frustrated can be seen in his constant attacks against illegal immigrants. He has successfully scapegoated immigrants as "murderers," "rapists," "criminals," and "gang members." He exudes a powerful sense of taking control and getting things done that people find hard to resist.

Add to this disturbing trend the results of a poll by the *Economist* that one in five young people believe the Holocaust is a myth.[7]

---

5. Roberts-Miller, "Rhetoric and Hitler."

6. Ott and Dickinson, *Twitter Presidency*, 1.

7. *Economist*, "One in Five."

Young people, frustrated by the actions of Israel and by Biden's continued support of Israel, are an easy target for Trump's performance rhetoric, his antihero persona, and his ability to hijack the facts into a series of lies designed to benefit him.

On the positive side, there are reasons for showing respect and attention to young people willing to express dissatisfaction with Israel's conduct in Gaza. While I am reluctant to assert that young people are coalescing around a new "peace movement" reminiscent of the "anti-war" movement during the Vietnam War, I am encouraged when any demo group stands against war. On this precise point, the young people may be smarter than the rest of the nation.

Cohen says, "Overall, Mr. Trump is winning 21% of young Biden '20 voters who sympathize more with Palestinians than Israel, while winning 12% of other young Biden '20 voters. In an even more striking sign of defections among his own supporters, Mr. Biden holds just a 64–24 lead among the young Biden '20 voters who say Israel is intentionally killing civilians, compared with an 84–88 lead among the Biden '20 voters who don't think Israel is intentionally killing civilians."[8]

Of course, US support of Israel is complicated by evangelical support of Israel, traditional support of Israel, and by a fear of terrorism of any kind.

One can only hope that young people turning to Trump for help in ending Israel's war in Gaza only conveys how deeply frustrated they are. The disturbing factors of rising anti-Semitism and increased belief that the Holocaust is a myth suggest we are losing ground in the social media age of propaganda, conspiracy theories, and demagogic rhetorical strategies.

I commend young people for opposing war. I am not as easily swayed by such responses that rely on simplicity, impulsivity, and demagoguery. Perhaps there is hope here for a new peace and nonviolent gospel in our country. I can only react in horror that young people would seriously turn to the one person I believe is the embodiment of sheer evil in America, Donald Trump.

Israel and the United States need to make a new commitment to restoring trust in working for peace, democracy, and the adjudication of the real needs of Palestinians in Gaza. This is no time to keep doing what we have always done in maintaining hegemonic control over others.

8. Cohen, "Biden's Support of Israel."

Yes, a Free and Fair Press Is Under Assault by Trump and MAGA

T HE First Amendment to the Constitution of the United States can't stay off the political hot seat. There's a bill now before the US Senate, known as the PRESS Act—the Protect Reporters from Exploitative State Spying Act—that would prevent the government from forcing journalists to reveal their sources.

There doesn't seem to be anything dangerous in the bill. The House of Representatives, in a rare display of nonpartisanship, approved the bill on a voice vote.

Neither does the First Amendment appear to invite confusion or hostility. Thomas Jefferson, author of the First Amendment, said, "Our liberty depends on the freedom of the press, and that cannot be limited without being lost."[1]

Now, Senator Tom Cotton (Republican, Arkansas) has blocked the Senate from passing the bill, contending the legislation could put national security in jeopardy. Cotton would be helped by a remedial course from the author of the First Amendment: "Where the press is free and every man able to read, all is safe."[2]

1. Jefferson, "Jefferson to James Currie."
2. Jefferson, "Jefferson to Charles Yancey."

Tom Cotton

Eschewing evidence for emotion, Cotton attacked the media as "liberal." "The liberal media doesn't deserve more protections," Cotton declared during a brief speech on the Senate floor. "The press badge doesn't make you better than the rest of America or put you above the law."[3] This, of course, isn't about a rational commitment on his part to any policy, and it has absolutely nothing to do with the bill's purpose in protecting all media from undue government pressure. Cotton, flashing his political prejudice resorts to hyperbole: "If recent history has taught us anything, it's that too many journalists are little more than left-wing activists who are, at best, ambivalent about America and who are cavalier about our security and the truth."[4]

Cotton claimed, "For several years, the media has conducted itself in a disgraceful manner and destroyed its reputation with the American people. Yet some in Congress, maybe the only institution less popular than the press, now want to give it more privileges."[5]

Somehow Cotton ignores the stellar record of outstanding reporting done by the daily newspapers in America since our founding. The *New York Times*, for instance, has won 133 Pulitzer Prizes from 1918 to 2018. This is not disgraceful reporting.

It's Open Season on the Press

While politicians often have complex and adversarial relations with the press, no president or party ever has made such an "enemy of the state" out of the press as Donald Trump, who has made attacks on the press a major part of the Republican Party platform.

Trump has filed a lawsuit against CBS over its *60 Minutes* interview with Kamala Harris. He frequently threatens to strip broadcasters of their licenses. At least fifteen times he has argued television networks should have their licenses revoked because they criticized him. Between September 1 and October 24, Reporters Without Borders found Trump insulted, attacked, or threatened the press at least 108 times.[6]

3. Irwin, "Cotton Blocks Federal Shield."
4. Cotton, "PRESS Act."
5. Irwin, "Cotton Blocks Federal Shield."
6. McShane, "Press Freedom Groups."

ABC News previously shocked the world by agreeing to a fifteen-million-dollar settlement with Trump, who complained news personality George Stephanopoulos defamed him by saying a jury had found Trump guilty of "rape" of E. Jean Carroll, while the jury found him guilty and ordered him to pay a judgment of $83.3 million to her for defamation based on a finding that the once and future president had sexually abused her.

Trump, the convicted sexual abuser, liar, and defamer, does not want to be known as a "rapist," even though sixty-nine women have accused him of various forms of sexual assault, from harassment to attempted rape.

The settlement with ABC News will add yet another layer of preemptive caution in truth-telling on the abuse Trump has and will perpetuate. It is staggering that the most notorious liar ever to inhabit the White House can extract a fifteen-million-dollar settlement from a national news organization because he says they lied about his lying.

Less than forty-eight hours before election day, Trump told a rally of his supporters he wouldn't mind if someone shot the journalists in front of him. "I have this piece of glass here, but all we have really over here is the fake news. And to get me, somebody would have to shoot through the fake news. And I don't mind that so much," he said.[7]

American trust in the media has dropped from a high of 72 percent in the 1970s, according to Gallup, to a current low of 32 percent.[8] This is not an indication that reporters are lazy, incompetent, ignorant, or a bunch of liars. It is the result of relentless "propaganda" spread by Trump and MAGA and his surrogates.

How did we go so quickly from freedom of the press to "fake news" in America? How did we go from trusting the press to hold our politicians accountable to a ragtag bunch of politicians who are liars, frauds, and unaccountable to anyone?

The words of Thomas Paine spring to mind: "I become irritated at the attempt to govern mankind by force and fraud, as if they were all knaves and fools."[9]

7. Daher, "Trump Says He Doesn't Mind."

8. Brenan, "Americans' Trust in Media."

9. Paine, *Rights of Man*.

The Threat Is Real

Political attacks on US-based journalists and news organizations pose an unprecedented threat to their safety and the integrity of information.

A survey from the International Center for Journalism highlights a disturbing tolerance for political bullying of the press in the land of the First Amendment. The findings show this is especially true among white male Republican voters.[10]

The ICFJ's survey found more than one-quarter (27 percent) of the Americans polled said they had often seen or heard a journalist being threatened, harassed, or abused online. And more than one-third (34 percent) said they believe it is appropriate for senior politicians and government officials to criticize journalists and news organizations.[11]

Yamiche Alcindor, the *PBS NewsHour* presidential affairs correspondent, interviewed Francois Pierre-Louis, whose parents brought him from Haiti in the 1970s. Pierre-Louis observed, "The American public doesn't understand that democracy is a fragile system that can wither away if you don't take care of it."[12]

Perhaps Americans are not aware of the spread of authoritarian and demagogic rulers in the rest of the world.

Freedom House, in its *Freedom in the World 2021* report, raised the alarm: "Even before 2020, Trump had presided over an accelerating decline in US freedom scores, driven in part by corruption and conflicts of interest in the administration."[13]

Moreover, around the world more countries had performed worse on various measures of freedom than had improved compared to any other point since 2005. Democracy itself, Freedom House observed, had been rendered vulnerable.

"The expansion of authoritarian rule, combined with fading and inconsistent presence of major democracies on the international stage, has had tangible effects on human life and security," they concluded.[14]

Put as starkly as I know how: an attack on the freedom of the press is an attack on democracy.

10. Posetti and Ejaz, "Attacks on Journalists."
11. Posetti and Ejaz, "Attacks on Journalists."
12. Alexander, "December 15, 2020."
13. Repucci and Slipowitz, "Freedom in the World."
14. Repucci and Slipowitz, "Freedom in the World."

According to the 2023 World Press Freedom Index—which evaluates the environment for journalism in one hundred and eighty countries and territories and is published on World Press Freedom Day—the situation is "very serious" in thirty-one countries, "difficult" in forty-two, "problematic" in fifty-five, and "good" or "satisfactory" in fifty-two countries. In other words, the environment for journalism is "bad" in seven out of ten countries and satisfactory in only three out of ten.[15]

For the sake of comparison relevant to the USA and the authoritarian rulers Trump emulates and worships, Russia ranks 148th and Hungary 85th. The United States, which always has prided herself on being the leading democracy in the world, now ranks 32nd, indicating a much higher level of danger for US media compared to the other two.

Attacks on the free press are of particular importance because the first institution an autocratic demagogue takes control of is the press.

Viktor Orban and Hungary

Thwarting the free press was Viktor Orban's first move in taking control of the government of Hungary. Orban, a right-wing hero among American conservatives, has been labeled a "press freedom predator" by RSF (Reporters Without Borders).

Orban's media empire controls about five hundred outlets and gets 85 percent of the state advertising revenue. Independent media are allowed in Hungary, but they are subject to political, economic, and regulatory pressures.

In Hungary, the government regularly accuses critical media of disseminating false information and of receiving funding from George Soros. Journalists critical of the government often are harassed online by ruling party supporters. They are attacked by trolls, flooding them with comments with many personal elements, especially to female journalists.

Anne Applebaum, author of *The Twilight of Democracy*, chronicles the seductive lure of authoritarianism. She tells the story of the consequences of authoritarian government and reflects, "Whether I like it or not, I am part of this story."[16] She points out that in Hungary and Poland, leaders who sought to undermine the free press did so through money and influence.

---

15. Vásquez et al., *Human Freedom Index*.
16. Applebaum, *Twilight of Democracy*, 11.

Orban has made the free press his personal propaganda machine and television stations pro-government outlets. This is known as "media capture." When a nation loses the distinction between education and propaganda, that nation is ripe for an authoritarian takeover. Think Fox News as the only news source available in the US.

The Press Is Not an Innocent Victim

The media, not exactly a vestal virgin here, bears some responsibility. MSNBC President Phil Griffin told the *Hill* he wished Trump complained about MSNBC because complaining about CNN is "like a promo for CNN all the time."[17]

What if US media were more honest about themselves and their enabling of Trump and his anti-media campaign? They pretend we have nothing to worry about while dealing with the most intense attack on the freedom of press in American history. Yes, we have something to worry about.

Their "soft denial" is subtle and turns them into Trump enablers. They pretend they can keep making "news" together, even though the freedom to do so is running out and the kitchen is filling up with smoke.

The media and Trump share identical desires: clicks, ratings, and profits. Their performative drama has become its own prime-time series, and both are enriched by it. As Brian Beutler argued, "The press is not a pro-democracy trade, it is a pro-media trade. By and large, it doesn't act as a guardian of civic norms and liberal institutions—except when press freedoms and access itself are at stake."[18]

There's a foreboding sense that the powerful media moguls, with their billions, are in cahoots with Trump. They think, like Trump's evangelical dupes, they eventually will be able to reign him in and control him. But they aren't paying attention to the man who wants to be a "dictator for one day" and then another and another and who frequently has expressed the desire to have a third term and then be president for life.

Communication theorist Paul J. Achter concludes, "That is their purpose, and there is no reason to think it will serve the needs of the American people."[19]

17. Concha, "Ratings on Rise."
18. Beutler, "Media Is Botching."
19. Achter, "Great Television," 126.

This moment of washing the dirty laundry of the media doesn't lessen the danger faced in attacks on freedom of the press. The really big losers here will be democracy and the people.

Trump is stacking his administration with Fox News personalities and billionaires. Imagine a media environment where government officials refuse to speak to journalists and journalists are forbidden to attend events. Imagine Fox News as the only government-sanctioned media in the USA.

Hit the Reset Button

Now is as good a time as any for the people to hit the reset button and recover some basic facts.

- The media are not our enemy.
- The press is not "fake."
- The press doesn't engage in telling endless lies.
- This is but one more attack on the First Amendment.
- It is the media's job to hold all politicians accountable.
- Defend the First Amendment.
- Believe in truth.

We can never return to the way things were before attacking the press became the template. If we do not make major changes soon, then our institutions, our political system, and our society may collapse during the next major war, pandemic, financial meltdown, or constitutional crisis.

Passing the PRESS Act is one small step toward protecting everything Americans hold dear.

In the meantime, we must harden our commitment to the freedoms of speech, press, and religion so they can withstand chronic anger and mistrust.

Even more so, it is imperative that ordinary citizens seek, search, investigate, read, and know the facts and the truth. We must be able to discern the truth from the lies. Historian David Blight is right: "Disinformation must be fought with good information."[20]

20. Blight, "'Lost Cause' Myth."

American Values and a Tale of Two Islands

I N A MOVE THAT is more publicity stunt than workable policy, President Donald Trump has ordered his administration to prepare to house tens of thousands of "criminal aliens" at the Navy base at Guantanamo Bay.

"We have 30,000 beds in Guantanamo to detain the worst criminal illegal aliens threatening the American people," he said. "Some of them are so bad we don't even trust the countries to hold them, because we don't want them coming back, so we're going to send them out to Guantanamo."[1]

Everything about this messaging is designed to evoke fear—of him, of his administration, of immigrants themselves. He has moved from talking about mass deportations to talking about mass imprisonments—a facility whose very name evokes the horrors of 9/11. Therefore, undocumented immigrants are treated as terrorists.

Immigrants are less likely to commit crimes than US citizens.

Trump has consistently labeled those who cross the southern border into the US as rapists, thugs, and murderers—a scare tactic not based anywhere in reality. Now, his MAGA followers are calling all undocumented immigrants—"illegal aliens," in their book—criminals. They are "criminals" because they entered the US without permission, even if they filed constitutionally allowed asylum claims.

1. Watson et al., "Guantanamo Bay."

Constant Outrage

Trump has a habit of getting people to relate to one thing he says to make a larger point. For example, he frequently claims migrant gangs are not really humans. As David Livingston Smith argues, this is the ancient practice of "dehumanization." He defines dehumanization as "the belief that some beings only appear human, but beneath the surface, they aren't human at all."[2]

While he has not said all migrants are animals, the American capacity to draw conclusions from an isolated example turns into the idea that "all migrants are animals." The tendency to universalize is almost inescapable when viewed emotionally.

The Trump machine produces emotion twenty-four hours a day. Americans are commanded to feel angry, slighted, unappreciated, and resentful. From the White House, Trump parlays these feelings into government actions.

Trump sees an illegal immigrant criminal at every bus stop. He has instructed ICE to go into churches and schools—unlikely hangouts for criminals—to take prisoners. He has been doing this since he first likened Mexican immigrants to "murderers and rapists."

At the inaugural prayer service, Episcopal Bishop Mariann Budde asked Trump to have mercy on immigrants. His snarky response: "She failed to mention the large number of illegal migrants that came into our country and killed people. Many were deposited from jails and mental institutions. It is a giant crime wave that is taking place in the USA."[3]

Like a tape-recorded message stuck on repeat, Trump keeps repeating the same lies. In the face of overwhelming evidence that violent crime in the USA is down and the statistical proof that immigrants are less likely to commit murder than white Americans, Trump keeps repeating his lies, and his followers believe him.

Now, his plan to house detained immigrants at Guantanamo Bay's US Navy Base is another emotional effort to continually cast all migrants as criminals.

Ben Wittes, editor of the legal website Lawfare, told NPR, "The name Guantanamo Bay to America signals terrorist detention. So it elevates the status of what are really routine immigration enforcement actions into

2. Smith, *Less than Human*, 4.

3. Trump, "She Failed to Mention."

something like holding major terrorist figures that signals, 'I'm going to bring back the big bad Guantanamo Bay for this.'"[4]

Talking about the "criminal element" has a perverse sound since the former party of "law and order" has ignored the criminal acts against our nation on January 6 and pardoned the criminals of murder and mayhem. Now, brown people are the "criminals" needing rounding up and impounding.

A Tale of Two Islands

In American history, two islands illustrate the better angels of our national soul that pull us toward freedom, equality, and mutual respect, versus the lower angels that pull us toward fear, anger, and violence. Those two places are Ellis Island and the base in Guantanamo Bay, Cuba.

America has an ideal mythology that equals that of the Greeks. A major part of our mythology is symbolized by the Statue of Liberty and Ellis Island in New York Harbor.

More than a century ago, Ellis Island became the global metaphor for freedom. Thus Emma Lazarus penned the poem that gave written iconography to American ideals:

> Give me your tired, your poor,
> Your huddled masses yearning to breathe free,
> The wretched refuse of your teeming shore.
> Send these, the homeless, tempest-tost to me,
> I lift my lamp beside the golden door!"[5]

Ellis Island opened to receive immigrants on January 1, 1892. An Irish family consisting of Annie Moore, a teenage girl, and her two younger brothers made history as the very first immigrants to be processed there. Over the next sixty-two years, more than twelve million immigrants arrived in the United States via Ellis Island.

In 1924, political nativists comprised of politicians and preachers (some of them Baptist fundamentalists) fanned the flames of nativism to demand restrictions on immigration. Lady Liberty's light dimmed from shore to shore as a literacy test, the Chinese Exclusion Act, the Alien Contract Labor Law, quota laws, and the National Origins Act stemmed the flow of newcomers.

4. Pfeiffer, "Migrant to Guantanamo."
5. Lazarus, "New Colossus," lines 10–14.

The lamp of liberty was replaced with a sign at every American port: "No Trespassing. Violators Will Be Shot." As a result, Ellis Island faded in American memory, but Lady Liberty still stood there as stark reminder of the angels of our better nature.

During World War II, Ellis Island became the opposite of her first purpose. Japanese, German, and Italian nationals suspected of being enemy aliens were brought there to be interred.

Our National Nightmare

If Ellis Island is our dream representing the better angels of our spirit, Guantanamo Bay is our national nightmare.

The location takes its name from Guantánamo Province at the southeastern end of Cuba. This is the only military base the United States has in a communist country.

Located on Guantanamo is a high-security prison, "Gitmo," that held terrorist suspects after the September 11, 2001, attacks. It has become a notorious symbol of US excesses during the "war on terror," including the brutal mistreatment of prisoners and detention of suspects for two decades without charge.

Even though Trump's proposed place to house immigrant detainees is on a different plot of land at the base, not at the terrorist prison, the name carries the same weight.

Unfortunately, this is not a new idea. Haitian refugees and Cuban asylum seekers were held at Guantanamo Bay by the Clinton administration. In 1994, as many as forty-five thousand migrants were held there. In 2005, the nonprofit Amnesty International called it "the gulag of our time."[6]

"The facility is decrepit. It's been falling apart. It's in disrepair," he said. "And, as a practical matter, the conditions that would be created if people went there would be so substandard that it would give people opportunities to file lawsuits around the conditions of their confinement while they're being deported."[7]

The sheer numbers make this move unfeasible. About 1.4 million people in the United States are known to have deportation orders issued against them. An estimated 11 million people are living in the United

6. CBS News, "Guantanamo."

7. Pfeiffer, "Migrants to Guantanamo."

States without legal status, according to a 2024 report by the Department of Homeland Security. ICE deported the largest number of people in a decade during fiscal year 2024, the last full fiscal year of Joe Biden's presidency.

There are not thirty thousand "hardened criminals" who are illegal immigrants, but there are far more than thirty thousand immigrants Trump says he will deport.

This is nothing more than a cruel publicity stunt. But with Trump, the mere threat is the point. As always, the cruelty is the point.

What History Will We Choose?

James Baldwin observed, "History . . . does not refer merely to the past. . . . History is literally present in all that we do."[8]

America's dream incarnated in Ellis Island and the Statue of Liberty collides with America's nightmare exposed in Guantanamo Bay and Gitmo prison.

One of my favorite songs is "Down There by the Train." The lines that reach the deepest in my soul are those that say there will be no more eye for an eye, when Judas himself will carry John Wilkes Booth. I want to add a single sentence: "I saw Martin King carrying Caesar Chavez." I believe looking out of the window of every American there is an Ellis Island and a Gitmo. Ellis is where we want to be. This is America's dream.

It is time to come home to Ellis Island and all the freedom and liberty the Lady possesses in her heart.

8. Grossman, "James Baldwin on History."

Trump and the Story of the Magical Phone App for Immigrants

DONALD TRUMP WANTS EVERYONE to believe immigrants are bad. The formula is simplistic, misleading, and false, but it is the sum total of his immigration policy.

The simplicity, the impulsivity, and the emotionalism make Trump so tempting:

1. Immigrants are bad.
2. Real Americans are white and good.
3. Only Trump can save good America from bad immigrants.

Somewhere in the recesses of Mar-a-Lago, there's a secret room where Donald Trump and Stephen Miller mix conspiracy theories, dark web stories, and complete lies into vicious attacks against immigrants. Trump not only takes unbelievable stories from the web—think Haitian immigrants eating the pets of white people in Springfield, Ohio—he also takes normal services provided by our government and turns them into lurid conspiracy theories.

Trump's Smartphone App Theory

In one of his more bizarre claims, Trump insists Vice President Kamala Harris has a secret application that illegal immigrants have on their smartphones. During a speech at Trump Tower on Thursday, September 26, Trump read straight from a prepared script to blame the Biden administration for a migrant crisis. And he said Harris is using a secret smartphone app to transport migrants to states critical to Trump's election chances.

He seems to have watched too many Harry Potter movies. Magical modes of transportation among wizards like Potter include "floo powder," and a "portkey." There is in the wizarding world a lot of magical teleportation.

The "portkey" for migrants, according to Trump, is an app on their smartphones. He is dreaming up tech-smart immigrants who are put on secret flights in secret passenger jets by Harris and sneaked into the states crucial for him if he is going to win the election. In Trump's mind, the really dumb cat-and-dog-eating migrants have been magically transformed into supersecret really smart high-tech invaders.

Apparently, Trump heard about the app provided by the US Customs and Border Protection (CBP) mobile application CBP One, launched in 2020. It is available on the Apple App and Google Play stores. The purpose of the app is to provide appropriate services for immigrants, and it has been criticized as clunky and inefficient.

In Trump's mind this was nothing but a way to help more illegal immigrants sneak into the country. "They have a phone app so that people can come into our country," Trump claimed. "These are smart immigrants, I guess because most people don't have any idea what the hell a phone app is. But they do, these are very intelligent immigrants."[1]

As stated on the CBP website, "CBP has performed a comprehensive review of its services to determine how we can successfully leverage emerging technology to add an extra layer of security and efficiency while supporting the travel recovery efforts."[2]

Trump concocted the rest of the story from thin air. He claims, "In addition, through her phone app, something totally new now, it's a phone app for migrants, where migrants call in. She's allowed them to press a button and schedule an appointment to be released into the interior of our county."[3]

Trump elaborated, "As president, I will immediately end the migrant invasion of America. We will stop all migrant flights, end all illegal entries, terminate the Kamala phone app for smuggling illegals [CBP

1. Mazza, "Baffling Claim."
2. US Customs and Border Protection, "Lawful Travel."
3. Leeson, "Phone App."

One App], revoke deportation immunity, suspend refugee resettlement and return Kamala's illegal migrants to their home countries [also known as remigration]. I will save our cities and towns in Minnesota, Wisconsin, Michigan, Pennsylvania, North Carolina, and all across America. MAGA2024!"[4]

The Trump Reversal

If you long ago stopped listening to Trump, you will not know his description of illegal immigrants has changed drastically. Now he tells people to pay no attention to his original lies that immigrants are criminals.

His old lie about immigrants was, "When Mexico sends its people, they're not sending their best. . . . They're sending people that have lots of problems and they're bringing those problems with them. They're bringing drugs. They're bringing crime. They're rapists."[5]

Immigrants have gone from being criminals who are dumber than dirt to being high-tech secret agents in cahoots with the vice president of the United States. Harris is an immigrant "mole" in the White House.

The Trump train has left the main track of American politics. Now, it is a runaway train endangering everyone. The strategy is clear: Make up any story. Tell as many lies as you can manufacture. Have your surrogates defend, repeat, and expand the lies. Bury the electorate in bluster.

Yet there's nothing new in Trump's immigration rants. If he had some new policy capable of helping deal with the immigration issue in positive and helpful ways, why does he resort to demagogic nativism attacks? Because he's got nothing.

Dismantling the Expectation of Truth-Telling

Here's what I believe is at stake: Trump has dismantled the fundamental expectation of truth-telling and good faith in America. Until the age of Trump, Americans assumed politicians were acting in good faith until there was definitive proof otherwise. Americans also assumed politicians would accept the value of truth and would act accordingly if they were caught lying.

4. Shaw, "Trump Reveals New Pledge."
5. McKay, "15 Head-Scratching Quotes."

When caught lying, the politician would leave office in shame and disgrace. Trump has changed all this. There is no longer a standard of truth-telling. Shamelessness has replaced shame.

When a Trump lie is exposed, if anything, he gains strength and influence. People are impressed he can say such outrageous and crazy stuff, get away with it, and still not lose any votes.

If anything, Trump escalates. When the report of Haitian immigrants eating cats and dogs was conclusively shown to be false, Trump and Vance didn't stop telling the lie. They escalated.

Trump's smartphone apps for the magic transportation of illegal immigrants to a swing state makes Marjorie Taylor Greene's "Jewish space lasers" look like the work of a kindergartner. This is the master class in humbuggery, foolishness, and, yes, stupidity.

The Framework of Populist Nativism

What is going on here? I think for Trump the entire game is wrapped in the framework of populist nativism. Label it Nativism.7 because America has spasmodic outbreaks of nativism—a movement where the white natives get scared and think the African Americans are going to steal their women, the Irish Catholics are going to destroy Protestant Christianity, the Chinese are going to take all the jobs, the Germans and the Japanese are our sworn enemies, and Black and brown people are coming from an array of what Trump calls "shit-hole countries."

Whenever three or more white males are afraid in America, a new nativist movement is born. Trump is dragging up nasty, discredited history from the garbage dump of Gehenna. He is carrying on an old family tradition rooted in nativist populism. Nativism is the frame of Trump's rhetoric. Trump is a populist in the paranoid tradition of such aberrations as Joseph McCarthy and Patrick Buchanan. America rejected McCarthy and Buchanan, but Buchanan is still important because of his influence on Trump.

In *State of Emergency: The Third World Invasion and Conquest of America*, Buchanan's anti-immigrant positions are clear and threatening. While it is doubtful Trump has ever read Buchanan, he imbibed his ideas.

For example, Buchanan said, "It needs to be said again: If we do not solve our civilizational crisis—a disintegrating culture, dying populations and invasions unresisted—the children born in 2006 will witness in their lifetimes the death of the West. In our hearts we know what must be done. We must stop the invasion. But do our leaders have the vision and the will to do it?"[6]

Buchanan had a plan for immigration:

+ Stop all immigration

+ Eliminate amnesty for immigrant workers

+ Build a permanent fence (Trump's wall)

+ No more "anchor babies"—no citizenship to babies born in the USA

+ Stop "chain migration"—family reunification policy

+ End dual citizenship

+ Remove the "magnets"—end the incentives for illegal immigrants

+ Remigration

Trump is Pat Buchanan in more expensive suits, a greater television persona, and a charismatic leadership style. Trump is Buchanan with makeup and lipstick and orange hair.

Here's a Better Story

Instead of drowning in Trump's rage, rhetorical scholar Robert L. Ivie says there needs to be an "affirming gesture of concurrence." There needs to be a picture "of partners, family, friends, neighbors, networks, the common good and other humanizing images of diversity, interdependence, mutual regard, mutual action, mutual influence and mutual benefit."[7]

A different story needs to be told. Not a made-up story like those of Trump and Vance but real-life stories of the value of immigrants to the American story.

There is a better, healthier, more truthful immigrant story. Heather McGee, in *The Sum of Us*, challenges Trump's apocalyptic vision of destroyed American cities and small towns by recounting how immigration has proved to be a win-win for locals as a means of repopulating and revitalizing small towns across the country.[8]

---

6. Buchanan, *State of Emergency*, 2.

7. Ivie, "Dissenting Democratically," 11.

8. McGee, *Sum of Us*, 243.

Trump says the governors and mayors are embarrassed to tell the truth about the devastation caused by immigrants. Listening to Trump, you would think illegal immigrants have invaded small towns like hordes of swarming locusts from the Old Testament.

It's a carefully packaged apocalyptic set of lies. Trump is sowing the seeds of racial division in an attempt to win the election. He is exploiting the fears of Americans who are anxious about a nation being created "with no racial majority."

Trump singled out Springfield, Ohio, for his big lie about immigrants. I offer a trip to Lewiston, Maine, as an alternative story. The secret to Lewiston's success: thousands of refugees from the Somali Civil War were resettled in the Atlanta suburbs of Georgia. Word of mouth got some to Portland and then to Lewiston, where the quiet streets offered more peace and the low rents more security. Soon other African refugees—from the Congo, Chad, Djibouti, and Sudan—moved to Lewiston. City planner Phil Nadeau said, "The refugee arrivals . . . are filling apartments that were vacant for a long time. They're filling storefronts on Lisbon Street that were vacant for a long time. They're contributing to the economy."[9]

Nadeau is passionate about the value of the "new Mainers," as he calls them, to the revitalization of Lewiston. He boasts that while other Maine small towns had plummeting real estate values, fleeing young people, and shuttering schools, Lewiston is building new schools—and creating the jobs that come with that. He can't say enough about the benefit of migration to small towns like his. A bipartisan think tank calculated that Maine's African immigrant households contributed $194 million in state and local taxes in 2018.

Immigrants are repopulating once-dying small towns. Pick a state, and you'll find this story in one corner or another. Kennett Square, Pennsylvania, is now 50 percent Latinx, mostly from Mexico, and it's a community given new life by the families of migrant workers at the local mushroom farms.

Towns across the Texas panhandle have been drying up and losing population for years, but the potato farming stronghold of Dalhart grew by 7 percent from 1990 to 2016 because of Latinx families. Once immigrants have moved to a small town, as European immigrants did

9. McGee, *Sum of Us*, 243.

a century ago, they start businesses, gain education, and participate in civic life.

According to McGee, a study of more than twenty-six hundred rural communities found that over the three decades after 1990, two-thirds lost population. However, immigration helped soften the blow in the majority of these places, and among the areas that gained population, one in five owes the entirety of its growth to immigration. In the decade after 2000, people of color made up nearly 83 percent of the growth in rural population in America.[10]

The Truth

Here's the bottom line, the honest-to-God truth: Trump is lying about what is happening to the small towns in the US. Trump's apocalyptic story is as full of holes as a premillennial evangelist going on about a fictional rapture. His vision is a dark, fearful, and distorted one.

Americans have a clear choice. We made this same choice when we rejected the nativism and anti-immigration of Buchanan. Now, we need to emphatically reject it again.

Trump has had his moment in the sun. Like a bad reality television show, it is time for him to recede into the shadows. As the unknown writer of Ecclesiastes knew, "For everything there is a season, and a time for every matter under heaven: . . . a time to break down, and a time to build up."[11]

In America, it is a time to laugh and dance in the glory of diversity and inclusion.

It is a time to throw away the misinformation and lies of Trump and keep the values of character and truthfulness.

It is time to tear down the wall of hatred, racism, and division and a time to stitch together the common good of Americans.

It is time to speak, to love, and to make peace.

It is a time to reject the dark apocalyptic language of Trump and embrace the newness of opportunity provided by so many different peoples and cultures.

10. McGee, *Sum of Us*, 244.
11. Eccl 3:1, 3 ESV.

Trumpism Is Leading America
to the Valley of Dry Bones

S OMETHING IS TERRIBLY WRONG in America. We are in a mess.
Perhaps even more disturbing is that there may be more people
wanting to wallow in the mess because they wish to profit from
our alienation from each other.

After watching Donald Trump's weekend rally in Waco, Texas, the
biblical story of the valley of bones is the best metaphor that came to
mind.

The *Hill* reported,

> Former President Trump started off his first official 2024 cam-
> paign rally on Saturday in Waco, Texas, with a rendition of "The
> Star-Spangled Banner" sung by a group of inmates that are incar-
> cerated for their role in the Jan. 6 Capitol riot. The song, called
> "Justice for All," features the defendants, who call themselves the
> J6 Choir, singing a version of the National Anthem and includes
> Trump reciting the Pledge of Allegiance over the track. Trump
> stood with his hand over his heart as the song played and as im-
> ages from the Capitol riot, in which Trump supporters stormed
> the complex to overturn the 2020 election, played on a screen.[1]

This at a rally set against the thirtieth anniversary of the FBI raid
on the breakaway Mormon sect, Branch Davidians, which also oc-
curred near Waco.

1. Neukam, "Trump Opens Campaign Rally."

Trump spoke in apocalyptic terms: "And 2024 is the final battle, it's going to be the big one. You put me back in the White House, their reign will be over and America will be a free nation once again."[2]

Learn from Ezekiel

We should learn from the message preached by Ezekiel to the children of Israel about what would happen to them unless they return to God. He paints a picture of a valley of dead bones: "The hand of the LORD came upon me, and he brought me out by the spirit of the LORD and set me down in the middle of a valley; it was full of bones. He led me all round them; there were very many lying in the valley, and they were very dry."[3]

America, too, is on the road to the valley of bones. Never forget that democracy can disappear in a fog of fascism and tyranny. We are losing our national consciousness.

"I'm an American" is being replaced with something smaller, more dangerous, more divisive, crueler.

This is not just about Trump; he's the carnival sideshow on the road to the valley of dry bones; he's the cipher in the mess for what's wrong. The key indicators are greed, a dependence on spectacles and entertainment to numb the pain of meaninglessness, escalating authoritarianism, and an aggressive military always prepared to throw its weight around.

All these evils dominate the American culture right here and right now. And we have lost all sense of proper empathy.

On the Road to Perdition

A parade of mini-Trumps and Trump wannabes—many spangled in religious rhetoric—are following this sideshow on the road to perdition.

Consider Minnesota State Senator Steve Drazkowski, who recently said children in his state aren't hungry enough to justify funding free meals at school. "I have yet to meet a person in Minnesota that is hungry," he said.[4]

Or Oklahoma State Representative Jim Olsen, who recently said the Bible endorses corporal punishment of disabled children.

2. Neukam, "Trump Opens Campaign Rally."

3. Ezek 37:1–2.

4. Gregorian, "DGOP State Legislator."

Or US Representative Marjorie Taylor Greene (Republican, Georgia), who recently spouted, "We need a national divorce. We need to separate by red states and blue states and shrink the federal government. Everyone I talk to says this."

Pressed on whether this was realistic, she added, "It's something we should work toward because it's kind of the vision that our Founding Fathers had for America, and I think it's great."[5]

She reminds me of Representative Preston Brooks of South Carolina, who beat Senator Charles Sumner of Massachusetts with a walking cane on May 22, 1856, in the United States Senate chamber. Brooks was not censored by the House of Representatives. Instead, he was reelected to the House by his constituents. Sumner was unable to return to the Senate for three years.

As described by historian Stephen Puleo, "The caning had a tremendous impact on the events that followed over the next four years: the increasing militancy of the abolitionist movement, the meteoric rise of the Republican Party, and the secession of the Southern states and the founding of the Confederacy. While Sumner eventually recovered, compromise had suffered a mortal blow and in its place came escalating tensions and violence. Puleo interprets the caning as the event that led to civil war.[6]

While her elected colleagues today seek to cane the poor, the disabled, the minority, and the immigrant, Greene proposes a rhetorical caning of our Constitution.

Greene will be ignored only by those who mistake her as a solo act rather than the soul of what has become today's Republican Party. As heretical as Christian nationalism has become, we need to know this was only the beginning. In less than a year, Greene has moved from promoting a government operated by Christians to an embrace of the Lost Cause of the Confederacy.

She was, of course, on the platform with Trump in Waco.

All this is an invitation to hell—or the valley of dry bones.

5. Pettypiece, "Marjorie Taylor Greene."
6. Puleo, Caning, xi.

We Are Attached

Like it or not, we are attached. We are the United States of America. We are one nation, and some even insist one nation under God. We are one people. No doubt a single political party could go to hell, but not without doing serious damage to the nation. We need each other.

It took Catholics and Protestants more than five centuries to understand neither of us has a story without the other, and some are still grumbling in their beer and bourbon about it.

What can preachers do? We can preach. In advance of our relentless march to the valley of dry bones, we can offer a different road. We can change our ways, change our minds, change our direction. We can make a U-turn and take a new road.

We also can turn to Scripture to remind us there may be a latent fascist waiting to emerge in all powerful politicians. This is why I read Isa 14 with Ezek 37. God said to Isaiah, "You will take up this taunt against the king of Babylon."[7] Isaiah obeys God and taunts the king. "O Day Star, son of Dawn! How you are cut down to the ground, you who laid the nations low! You said in your heart, 'I will ascend to heaven; I will raise my throne above the stars of God; I will sit on the mount of assembly on the heights of Zaphon; I will ascend to the tops of the clouds, I will make myself like the Most High.' But you are brought down to Sheol, to the depths of the Pit."[8]

Nebuchadnezzar went from the penthouse to the outhouse. He went from ruling the world to eating grass. He went from incredible riches to abject poverty. People scorned him, mocked him, and derided him. In modern parlance, "Who is this punk who once made the earth tremble, who shook kingdoms?"

The warning is not just for Donald Trump; it is for us. If we don't wake up, we are going to end up in the valley of dry bones.

American historian Timothy Snyder, in *On Tyranny*, advises us: Do not obey a voice of charisma and power without thinking about what he or she is saying. Do not obey the voice in advance. Take responsibility for the face of the world beginning in your local neighborhood because all politics is local. And defend and maintain ethics.[9]

---

7. Isa 14:4.

8. Isa 14:12–15.

9. Snyder, *On Tyranny*, 5–6.

Why? Because character still matters. Believe in truth; pursue it, follow it, keep it. Listen for dangerous words and refuse to follow the slinger of such words. Keep your cool when the unthinkable happens. Be a patriot in its deepest, truest sense. The true patriot carries on a love argument with the nation.

True Patriotism

And a true patriot is not motivated by greed or selfishness—the stock-in-trade of Trumpism.

Greed perpetuates a world of scarcity—a world suspicious that showing too much empathy will not leave enough for the privileged. As the prophets preached, empathy must be acted upon, not just spoken of. A liberal who insists on empathy in every area of human life but never takes any action is a person who only uses empathy as a weapon against conservatives.

Empathy is a strong moral value that requires the responsibility, the courage, the will, and the strength to act.

At Root, This Is What Is Missing from Trump and Trumpism

Fortunately for all humanity, Jesus showed us another way. Perhaps no one has ever expressed it with such power as the apostle Paul, who said Jesus, "though he was in the form of God, did not regard equality with God as something to be exploited, but emptied himself, taking the form of a slave, being born in human likeness. And being found in human form, he humbled himself and became obedient to the point of death—even death on a cross."[10]

This is the empathy that should structure all of human life, including our government. There's no such thing as too much empathy. It is the lack of empathy—replaced by vanity—that hurts us the most and leads us to the valley of dry bones.

10. Phil 2:6–8.

Edwin Edwards and Louisiana Taught Donald Trump and MAGA How to Dance with the Devil

A s I watched the announcement of Donald Trump's conviction on thirty-four felony counts May 30, I thought to myself, "I've seen this show before."

Indeed, I was living in Louisiana in 2001 when Governor Edwin Edwards was convicted of racketeering and sent to federal prison. The parallels between Trump and Edwards are remarkably strong.

Louisiana may lead the nation in elected officials doing time for crimes. Since 1980, seventy-one Louisiana politicians have been convicted of an array of crimes. Even when our colorful politicians didn't go to jail, we have been tainted by scandal.

Many Louisiana residents have long reveled in our state's reputation for crooked politicians. The sheriff of Avoyelles Parish was reelected to his job while serving time in his own jail for malfeasance in office.

A movie was made of "Uncle Earl" Long's sexual liaisons with New Orleans stripper Blaze Starr. Ted Jones, an eighty-one-year-old former aide to Long, said after Starr's death, "Of course, Ms. Blanche [Long's wife] didn't like her, but that was beside the point. . . . It didn't mar his legacy; it demonstrated that old men have a flair for nice women."[1]

Democratic US Representative William Jefferson's Congressional office was raided on August 3, 2005. During a later raid of his home, FBI agents found ninety thousand dollars of cash in a freezer, wrapped in

---

1. Associated Press, "Blaze Starr."

aluminum foil and stuffed inside frozen-food containers. Jefferson gave literal meaning to the idea of "cold, hard cash."

Edwin "Fast Eddy" Edwards was raised a Roman Catholic and preached in the Church of the Nazarene as a teen. He didn't drink or smoke. Despite his unabashed fondness for high-stakes gambling, dirty jokes, and his reputation as a womanizer, he earned a following among Catholics and fundamentalists.

After one of his winning races for governor, Edwards paid off his debts from the fourteen-million-dollar campaign by chartering a ten-thousand-dollar-a-head trip to France for his friends and supporters. "I've wanted all my life to be a king, and now I can be," he quipped during their stop in Versailles.

The *New York Times* said of Edwards, "He served four terms, charmed voters with his escapades and survived a score of investigations before going to prison in 2002 for racketeering."[2]

Before There Was Donald Trump, There Was Edwin Edwards

Louisiana loved Edwards—charismatic, intelligent, humorous, political genius, easy to relate to, and with a sense of being the common man. Edwards may have been the greatest political quipster since Winston Churchill: "As you know, they sent me to prison for life," he told them. "But I came back with a wife."[3] When questioned about illegal campaign contributions, Edward replied, "It was illegal for them to give, but not for me to receive."[4]

For decades, Edwards was the target of criminal investigations that went nowhere. He acknowledged being questioned by twenty-two state and federal grand juries—about selling state jobs to campaign contributors, about a ten-thousand-dollar "gift" to his wife from a Korean businessman, and about paying gambling debts with cash of unknown origin. "Fast Eddie" shrugged it all off.

2. McFadden, "Edwin Edwards."
3. McFadden, "Edwin Edwards."
4. Bridges, "Edwin Edwards."

Edwards had a shameless attitude displayed proudly in public. He said, "Two out of 10 women will go to bed with you, but you've got to ask the other eight."[5] And indeed he won again.

Before election day, Edwards joked with reporters, "The only way I can lose this election is if I'm caught in bed with either a dead girl or a live boy."[6] Edwards zinged his opponent many times, once describing him as "so slow it takes him an hour and a half to watch *60 Minutes*." During a gubernatorial debate in 1983, his opponent asked Edwards, "How come you talk out of both sides of your mouth?" Edwards instantly responded, "So people like you with only half a brain can understand me."[7]

In February 1985, soon after his third term began, Edwards was forced to stand trial on charges of mail fraud, obstruction of justice, and bribery, brought by US Attorney John Volz. The charges were centered on an alleged scheme in which Edwards and his associates received almost two million dollars in exchange for granting preferential treatment to companies dealing with state hospitals. Edwards proclaimed his innocence and insisted the charges were politically motivated by his opponents.

The first trial resulted in a mistrial in December 1985, and a second trial in 1986 resulted in an acquittal. After Edwards and his four co-defendants were acquitted, the hotel where the jurors had been sequestered revealed that half the jurors had stolen towels as they left. Edwards quipped that he had been judged by a "jury of my peers."[8]

The trials were a circus, and at one point during the first trial but before the mistrial, Edwards rode to the Hale Boggs US Courthouse on a mule from his hotel. When asked by reporters why he did so, he replied something to the effect that it was symbolic of the speed and intellect of the federal judicial system, but also that he supported "tradition."

Marion Edwards, his attorney, often wore a pinstripe suit with a top hat and cane and held comedic press briefings at the end of each court session on the steps of the courthouse. Marion Edwards mocked the US Department of Justice, US Attorney John Volz, and Federal Judge Marcel Livaudais, who presided over the trials.

5. Maginnis, "Last Populist."
6. McGaughy, "Edwin Edwards' Best Quotes."
7. McGaughy, "Edwin Edwards' Best Quotes."
8. Carville and Hunt, "Death of a Legend."

For my money, Edwards was smarter, slicker, savvier, and funnier than Trump, but Edwards and Louisiana taught Trump and MAGA how to dance with the devil.

Edwards and David Duke

Edwards was elected governor of Louisiana for a fourth time when he defeated David Duke, a former grand wizard of the Ku Klux Klan. Edwards said, "While David Duke was burning crosses and scaring people, I was building hospitals to heal them."[9] A popular bumper sticker urging support for Edwards read, "Vote for the Crook. It's Important."

Edwards said of Duke that "the only thing we have in common is that we both have been wizards beneath the sheets" and feigned concern for Duke's health due to smoke inhalation "because he's around so many burning crosses."[10]

When a reporter asked Edwards what he needed to do to triumph over Duke, Edwards replied, "Stay alive."[11] On election day, Edwards defeated Duke in a landslide, 61 percent to 39 percent, a margin of nearly four hundred thousand votes.

Edwards Convicted of Bribery

After his fourth term, Edwards was indicted in 1998 by the federal government with the prosecution led by US Attorney Eddie Jordan. Edwards, the high roller of Las Vegas, finally was convicted on charges of taking bribes from gambling interests for licenses for riverboat casinos.

Edwards was found guilty on seventeen of twenty-six counts, including racketeering, extortion, money laundering, mail fraud, and wire fraud. Edwards seemed unfazed: "I did not do anything wrong as a governor, even if you accept the verdict as it is, it doesn't indicate that."[12]

On his way to prison he said, "I will be a model prisoner, as I have been a model citizen."[13] Governor Edwards became inmate number 03128–95.

9. Capitol News Bureau, "22 Edwin Edwards Quotes."
10. Carville and Hunt, "Death of a Legend."
11. Liquisearch, "Edwin Edwards."
12. Capitol News Bureau, "22 Edwin Edwards Quotes."
13. Capitol News Bureau, "22 Edwin Edwards Quotes."

In a poll taken in October 2011, months after he had been released from prison, 30 percent of respondents named Edwards the state's best governor since 1980. Bad boy, gambler, womanizer, convicted felon, Edwards still was the king of Louisiana.

Donald Trump May Face the Same Fate

Although time will tell. Trump said, while leaving the courthouse, the real verdict will be delivered by the American people November 5—in an election he may not be able to vote in as a convicted felon. But in an irony that would make Louisiana proud, convicted felons are not barred from serving as president.

For now, we are witnesses to history. Trump is the first president ever put on trial for criminal charges. No matter how much of a circus the trial has been, it is an unprecedented event in American history.

Will any of this matter to the voters? Even his supporters have long known Trump was a convicted liar, yet they supported him. They knew he was guilty of defrauding students in the Trump University case. No problem. They supported him. They knew he defrauded vendors and business partners, but no worry, that's just business. They knew he survived two impeachment trials only because he had a Republican majority in the Senate, but that's just politics.

No populist ever has attracted Trump's level of support in the United States. He could have used that for good, but he has chosen a different path. A path fueled by his arrogance, greed, and disdain for the rule of law.

Will he go to prison? Will he be elected president again? It's too early to tell. Things that would instantly destroy any other politician only make him more popular with his base. Like a good politician from Louisiana, don't count him out.

Having cast my vote for Edwards, the crook, in 1991, I realize many Americans may make the same decision even after Trump has become a convicted felon.

No Crystal Ball Needed to See a
Second Trump Term: Look at Israel

T HERE'S ALREADY A CLEAR picture of what a second Donald
Trump presidency would entail: just look at Israeli Prime
Minister Benjamin Netanyahu.

Yossi Klein Halevi, in the article "Netanyahu's Betrayal of Democracy Is a Betrayal of Israel," provides a stark picture of Netanyahu's hubris and greed.

Halevi is a senior fellow at the Shalom Hartman Institute where he is codirector, together with Imam Abdullah Antepli of Duke University and Maital Friedman of the Muslim Leadership Initiative, and a member of the Institute's iEngage Project. His latest book, *Letters to My Palestinian Neighbor*, is a *New York Times* bestseller. His previous book, *Like Dreamers*, was named the 2013 National Jewish Book Council Book of the Year.

A raft of articles has speculated on a second Trump term based on what Trump has been saying at his rallies and in his social media posts.

For example, Jonathan Rauch, in "Trump's Second Term Would Look Like This," in the *Atlantic*, warns, "A second Trump term could bring about the extinction of American democracy. Essential features of the system, including the rule of law, honest vote tallies and orderly succession, would be at risk."[1]

He expects Trump will "install toadies in key positions"; "intimidate the career bureaucracy" with loyalty tests; "co-opt the armed forces" because Trump believes the military was a source of resistance in his first

---

1. Rauch, "Trump's Second Term."

term; take full control of the judiciary; "weaponize the pardon"; and "defy court orders."[2]

What I propose here moves away from political speculation and from too much attention to Trump's rhetoric, to an inside look at how Netanyahu governs Israel. Here is the picture of a second Trump administration clearly revealed.

The Criminality of Netanyahu and Trump

As Halevi demonstrates, no Israeli government has had more ministers convicted of crimes or under indictment than Netanyahu's.

"As for Netanyahu, only a man who no longer cares about the dignity and good name of Israel could have brought the most extreme elements of society into the inner sanctum of government," Halevi writes. "The Netanyahu government is the most politically extreme, the most morally corrupt, and the most contemptuous of good governance in Israel's history. We have known governments with extremist elements, governments rife with corruption or incompetence, but not all at once and not to this extent."[3]

Like Netanyahu, Trump has brought far-right radicals into the mainstream of government and will populate the "Swamp" with even more in a second term. His corruption is mind-numbing. His greed and selfishness know nothing of boundaries. Trump always puts his interests above those of America and his own followers in every case.

No other president ever has brought such a reviled group from the right fringe of our politics into the center of power. Trump allies already sentenced to prison are doing so after being found guilty of various crimes, including campaign finance violations and lying to Congress. The list includes former White House Chief Strategist Steve Bannon, former Trump lawyer and "fixer" Michael Cohen, campaign co-chairs Rick Gates and Paul Manafort, former Trump administration trade official Peter Navarro, former campaign advisor George Papadopoulos, and longtime Trump confidant and far-right lobbyist Roger Stone.

2. Rauch, "Trump's Second Term."
3. Halevi, "Netanyahu's Betrayal."

The Mortal Danger of the Political/
Religious Alliance

Halevi argues Netanyahu's greatest liability is the deal he brokered with the far-right religious movement in Israel.

He says, "This government that speaks in the name of the Torah desecrates the name of Judaism. This government that speaks in the name of the Jewish people risks tearing apart the relationship between Israel and the Jewish diaspora. This government that speaks in the name of the Israeli ethos is the greatest threat to the ethos that binds Israelis together. This government that speaks in the name of Israeli security is a gift to those seeking to isolate the Jewish state and portray it as criminal."[4]

Trump speaks in the name of the Bible proclaimed by evangelical Christians in the US, but his words desecrate the name of Christianity. The rhetoric of Donald Trump that speaks in the name of the American people risks tearing apart the relationships between fellow Americans. Trump is the greatest threat to the ethos that binds Americans together.

The Disregard for the Anchor
Institutions of Democracy

Halevi points out no other prime minister's administration has had such disregard for Israel's national institutions, dismantling ministries and distributing the pieces like spoils of war. No other government has shown such disdain for basic standards of decency. No other government has declared war on the judicial system, which even the US lawyer Alan Dershowitz, a Netanyahu ally, has called the gold standard that should not be tampered with.

The open contempt for the political system that Netanyahu and his Likud Party colleagues in the Knesset have displayed over the past year—boycotting the Parliament's committees and turning plenary sessions into staged scenes of mockery, encouraging thugs to harass the families of right-wing Knesset members who dared join the previous Bennett-Lapid government—was a mere rehearsal for the current assault on the nation's institutions.

In the US, Republicans have censored members of their own party for refusing to kowtow to Trump or for voting to impeach Trump. They

4. Halevi, "Netanyahu's Betrayal."

have mocked, insulted, and demeaned members of the Democratic leadership with unrelenting fury. Trump and his surrogates have attacked the Department of Justice, the courts, the judges, the family members of judges, and witnesses testifying against Trump.

A Mistaken Religious Identity Endangers Both Nations

Halevi says, "Most Israeli Jews . . . regard the state's Jewish identity as fundamental to its existence, perhaps even more than its democratic identity. . . . An Israel stripped of its Jewishness would lose its reason for being, its internal cohesion and the vitality that has enabled it to survive in a region hostile to its existence."[5]

Netanyahu presented voters with a stark—and utterly false—dichotomy between his "Jewish" camp and his opponents' "democratic" camp. The opposition's campaign to save democracy will fail so long as substantial parts of the public are convinced that *the left*—Netanyahu's all-purpose term for his opponents, most of whom in fact are centrists—is more committed to Israel's democratic identity than to its Jewishness.

Trump and the Evangelicals claim to be the "Christian" camp and their opponents the "Democratic" camp. Even if Evangelicals thought Trump was a criminal, a serial liar, and a cheat, they still would vote for him because they believe he is the Christian alternative to what they perceive as pagan Democrats. Robert Jeffress says Trump is the most "pro-family, Christian-friendly president" in our nation's history.[6]

Evangelicals have attempted to claim a monopoly on loyalty to their definition of Christianity. Opposing this in the name of democracy alone will only strengthen Trump's argument that the Democrats care little for America's Christian identity. Along with defending democracy, we must also challenge the evangelical claim to be protecting the nation's Christian identity. Mike Johnson's "biblical worldview" needs exposing as the farce it really is.

5. Halevi, "Netanyahu's Betrayal."
6. Young, "Robert Jefress' Excuses."

As Halevi notes, "If Netanyahu is allowed to claim a monopoly on loyalty to Jewishness, opposing this government in the name of democracy alone will only strengthen his argument that the rival camp cares little for Israel's Jewish identity. Along with defending our democratic institutions from assault, we must challenge the Netanyahu coalition's claim to be protecting the nation's Jewish identity."[7]

Hate and Fear Will Not Sustain a Democracy

Trump preaches a message of fear: Democrats hate America. They hate us. The argument: Democrats care little for America's Christian identity.

We must challenge the claim that only Republicans are protecting the nation's Christian identity. I am not sure we have grasped how much Evangelicals have convinced many Americans that we are the devil, the enemy of faith and state.

Halevi argues, "The question the centrist camp must place before the Israeli public is this: Should the Jewishness of the state of Israel be defined by rabbinic law or by the Zionist understanding of peoplehood? Framed that way, a decisive majority will side with the center. By salvaging the classical-Zionist vision of a Jewish state, we can help save Israeli democracy."[8]

I am convinced this is a valid argument for us as well. Our nation should not be defined by evangelical law, but by the deep understanding of the true nature of a democracy not saddled with a religious identity. Americans are not more Christian by being more nationalist.

I agree with Halevi asserting the danger of a movement based on fear. He says, "Like many Israelis, I am heartbroken by the self-inflicted wound of this extremist new government—and I am deeply afraid of the consequences. This coalition, united only by hatred and vengeance toward internal enemies, cannot possibly cope with the threats facing Israel. Sooner or later, the coalition will unravel. The nature of hatred is to undermine itself, eventually turning its own proponents against one another. I believe that the sanity and decency of Israel will endure. The question will be at what price."[9]

Trump and his allies are united only by hatred and vengeance toward internal enemies—fellow Americans now branded as devils, demons, insane, stupid, crazy, and dangerous. The nature of hatred is to undermine itself. Hatred doesn't possess the emotional power to sustain a nation.

---

7. Halevi, "Netanyahu's Betrayal."

8. Halevi, "Netanyahu's Betrayal."

9. Halevi, "Netanyahu's Betrayal."

Progressives have the language skills to speak with deep pathos of our love, but we have been hesitant because such language may sound in our ears like a perverted patriotism. But we can love America without forsaking the faith. And when someone you love is in danger, you draw closer, even if the threat is self-inflicted.

Every day Netanyahu shows us what a second Trump term will look like and how it will act. Netanyahu refuses to make peace with Hamas because his right-right religious supporters will desert him and he will no longer be the prime minister. In his selfish eyes, war is a better alternative, and the future of Israel and the Jewish people is secondary.

Never for a moment believe Trump cares for his followers. He only cares how many people he can use to maintain his own grasp on power.

Trump's Groundhog Day, the Insurrection That Refuses to Stop

I PLANNED TO WRITE THIS essay about January 6 as an anniversary piece. Because I am a public speech teacher, it has felt particularly cruel for conservatives to deny what happened on that dark day. When Donald Trump Jr. sarcastically invited people to celebrate the third anniversary of the "fake insurrection," I determined an anniversary piece would be too mild.

I have become convinced that January 6 was not a "sideshow" of Trump politics as usual. The Trump insurrection turns out not to be a "one and done" moment. Every morning, Trump is the lead actor in his own version of *Groundhog Day*.

He is still running to win the 2020 election. He is still inciting an insurrection. He keeps repeating the threatening parts of his January 6 speech at every rally.

Trump's January 6 speech offended and disregarded every presidential norm, tradition, and integrity. He might as well set fire to our flag and trample on it.

Ben Blanchet's article, "Trump Calls on Supporters to Stop 'Bags of Crap' Who Enter Polling Places," convinced me that January 6, 2024, was not an anniversary as much as a continuation. "At a rally in Mason City, Iowa, Trump echoed his false claims that the 2020 election had been stolen from him through tactics like ballot stuffing, and said that 'we're not going to let it happen again.' Trump said at the rally: 'We will fight for America like no one has ever fought before.'"[1]

1. Blanchet, "Trump Calls on Supporters."

Trump repeated his false claims that the 2020 election had been stolen from him and said, "We're not going to let it happen again."[2] The key here is that Trump repeats his January 6 insurrection speech. He added, "You should all stay in those voting booths. You should stay there and watch it. If you see bags of crap coming into the voting areas, you've got to stop it. You can't let it happen, because these guys are crooked as hell. They know how to cheat."[3]

In defense of the bathroom humor and awful language found here, I also point the reader to Leviticus, where issues of uncleanness dominate chapter 15. Moses holds back nothing: "When any man has a discharge from his member, his discharge makes him unclean."[4]

Listening to Trump, I, like Burke, have "a horrified sense of being gagged (To think that our children's destiny is in the hands of so dingy a priesthood!)"[5] There is a pungent odor, sometimes so strong as to become stifling. Our troubles are spreading from sources such as these. The overpowering stench of Trump's rhetoric mingles with the overpowering "crookedness" of the political, arresting the usual smooth, unconscious process of breathing in and breathing out.

Donald Trump has rallied Republican voters to go to the polls on election day, stake out all the local precincts, and be on the lookout for "bags of crap." This would be hilarious if it were part of a comedy routine. But this is a serious speech from the man favored to win the Republican nomination for president.

Trump is not using hyperbole. He is not "telling it like it is." He is not just "Trump being Trump." And he is not telling the truth. This is delusional, crazy, stupid stuff.

Holding my nose, trying to breathe normally, I too am all "gaspo, gulpo, gaggo" in the attempt to analyze Trump's smelly rhetoric. Kenneth Burke's "gulpo-gaggo-gaspo" reminded him of the breath-taking nature of the current political mess: "Nor do we ever for a moment overlook the breath-taking nature of the current political gagging."[6]

2. Blanchet, "Trump Calls on Supporters."

3. Blanchet, "Trump Calls on Supporters."

4. Lev 15:2.

5. Kenneth Burke, cited in Hawhee, *Moving Bodies*, 132.

6. Hawhee, *Moving Bodies*, 132.

Trump's galling disregard for democratic norms makes me feel like Burke as I witness the crookedness of our political hacks—"To think that our children's destiny is in the hands of so dingy a priesthood."

Questions multiply. Since when did a candidate for the White House refer to fellow Americans as a "bag of crap"? Presidential speeches riddled with hyperbole, misinformation, lies, and incoherent claims are not the norm. Using negative rhetorical strategies to whip huge crowds into a frenzy is not in the job description of a reasonable president.

How to define a bag of crap? Dog owners take their dogs for early morning walks. They carry little bags with them with a pooper scooper. They pick up the dog's crap and put it in the bag. That is a bag of crap. How do you ID a person as a "bag of crap?" Will it be the smell? The kind of clothes? Will it be the color of the skin? Will it be a sneaky look on the face? More than eighty million people voted for President Biden. How will Trump supporters know who is a "bag of crap?"

"How Will Trump Supporters Know Who Is a 'Bag of Crap?'"

I'm serious. If poll watchers are going to identify "bags of crap," they need an artist's sketch, a list of characteristics, a description of the suspects. And what if the poll watchers, and this is a real possibility, identify a fellow Magadonian as a "bag of crap"?

A brief review of Trump's January 6 speech provides more than enough evidence for this being a continuation of insurrection. Trump said then, "We will never give up, we will never concede. It doesn't happen. You don't concede when there's theft involved. . . . Our country has had enough. We will not take it any more and that's what this is all about. And to use a favorite term that all of you people really came up with: We will stop the steal."[7]

A Major Theme of Trump's Speech: "Fight for Trump!"

There are lines of the speech that seem to suggest a call for the crowd to takes matters into their own hands to correct this injustice through a more active or violent approach:

7. NPR, "Jan. 6 Speech."

- "We will not let them silence your voices. We're not going to let it happen. Not going to let it happen."

- "Our country has had enough. We will not take it any more and that's what this is all about. To use a favorite term that all of you people really came up with: We will stop the steal."

- "That's what they've done and what they're doing. We will never give up. We will never concede, it doesn't happen. You don't concede when there's theft involved."

- "When you catch somebody in a fraud, you're allowed to go by very different rules."

- "This is a time for strength. . . . It's all part of the comprehensive assault on our democracy and the American people to finally standing up and saying, 'No.' This crowd is again a testament to it."

- "We will not be intimidated into accepting the hoaxes and the lies that we've been forced to believe over the past several weeks. We've amassed overwhelming evidence about a fake election."

- "We're going to see whether or not we have great and courageous leaders or whether or not we have leaders that should be ashamed of themselves throughout history, throughout eternity, they'll be ashamed. And you know what? If they do the wrong thing, we should never ever forget that they did. Never forget. We should never ever forget."[8]

In Iowa, just days before the third anniversary of January 6, Trump shouted, "The radical left Democrats rigged the presidential election in 2020, and we're not going to allow them to rig the presidential election in 2024. Not going to allow that."[9] But here's the deal: it is happening again.

In full January 6 rhetorical battle gear, Trump said to his supporters in Mason City, "We will fight for America like no one has ever fought before." Trump then said, "2024 is our final battle."

In Donald Trump's world, every day is January 6.

---

8. Quotes from the speech are drawn from NPR, "Jan. 6 Speech."
9. Trump, "Sioux Center."

No, Mr. Trump, America Is
Not Going to Hell

AFTER DONALD TRUMP'S CONVICTION in his Manhattan trial, he said, "Our whole country is being rigged" and "has gone to hell." Then he added, "We're a nation in decline, serious decline. Millions and millions of people, pouring into our country right now, from prisons and from mental institutions, terrorists. And they're taking over our country."[1]

In contrast, Trump said, "I'm a very innocent man. And it's OK. I'm fighting for our country. I'm fighting for our Constitution."[2]

Trump has been saying "America is going to hell" since he first announced a run for the presidency in 2015. At Trump Tower that day he said, "When Mexico sends its people, they're not sending their best. . . . They're sending people that have lots of problems and they're bringing those problems with [them]. They're bringing drugs. They're bringing crime. They're rapists."[3]

Of all the lies, misinformation, and false claims made by Trump, only one stands out as the critical lynch pin of his movement: America is going to hell, and Democrats are greasing the skids.

Thinking of a credible defense against the claim of America going to hell, my analogical imagination recalled the famous essay by one of the editors of the *Sun*, Francis Pharcellus Church, "Is There a Santa Claus?"[4]

1. Asher, "Trump Unleashes."
2. Ramirez, "Trump Rants."
3. McKay, "15 Head-Scratching Quotes."
4. Church, "Is There a Santa Claus?"

I found his response to eight-year-old Virginia the best possible framework for a response to the proponents of "America is going to hell."

No, Mr. Ex-President, convicted felon, serial liar, our nation is not
going to hell. Many of the very people who support you testify to the
reality our nation is not a loser, a pathetic, third-rate nation on the skids
to hell. These Americans go to work every day, send their children to
school, support their communities, pay their taxes, and go to church on
Sunday. They are good neighbors to everyone. They are open to diversity,
inclusion, and acceptance. They will give the shirt off their back, go the
second mile, forgive, and offer reconciliation to others.

The nineteenth-century Social Gospel vision still lives in my heart.
I relish still the words of Katharine Lee Bates in "America the Beautiful."
Particular phrases ring true for me: "Crown thy good with brotherhood
from sea to shining sea!"; "God mend thine every flaw, confirm thy soul
in self-control, thy liberty in law"; "Who more than self their country
loved"; "May God thy gold refine till all success be nobleness and every
gain divine!"; "Crown thy good with brotherhood" and sisterhood; "God
shed his grace on thee"; "Till selfish gain no longer stain the banner of
the free!"[5]

From the evangelical preachers preaching America's doom and the
return of Jesus just around the corner, to Trump's "midnight in America"
rhetoric, I resist all this doom and gloom. I still prefer the instructions of
Saint Paul in Phil 4: "Whatever is true, whatever is honorable, whatever
is just, whatever is pure, whatever is pleasing, whatever is commendable,
if there is any excellence and if there is anything worthy of praise, think
about these things. Keep on doing the things that you have learned and
received and heard and seen in me, and the God of peace will be with
you."[6]

Donald Trump and his evangelical friends are wrong. They have
been afflicted by the ideology of a dark skepticism about the future of our
great nation. They do not believe unless they are in charge of what passes
for true belief. They think nothing can be which is not comprehensible
by their little minds.

All minds in our universe are little. In this great universe of ours,
carefully brought into the fullness of life by the slow, immeasurable
patience and persuasion of Almighty God, we are but God's creatures

5. Bates, "America the Beautiful."
6. Phil 4:8–9.

formed from the dust of the earth to praise him. Measured by the infinite wisdom of the universe around us, the tiny minds of Evangelicals are but a blip on time's radar. They are like chaff scattered by the wind.

Don't be afraid. America is not going to hell. America will continue to exist as a great nation for reasons secular and spiritual. I have confidence in our exuberant capitalism to keep the profits flowing. Even as the Evangelicals eviscerate the greed of our nation, they dip their wicks in the profits as much as the churches always have. The "hawkers of holiness" are as attracted to riches as Donald Trump is to gilded gold.

The Prediction of Hell an Old Story

Our demise by preachers addicted to riches is a story both old and new. The idea of America going to hell is also as old as the Puritans who came to our shores long before there was a United States of America. They were convinced America was going to hell before it could make a decent start.

Yes, our nation, now as always, faces immense challenges. There are signs of an increasing secular nation more interested in "flourishing" than in Christian faith. These signs are not indicators of our impending doom. And Evangelicals often conjure false causes for our declension: gay rights, abortion, feminists, the ACLU, socialists, liberals, Democrats.

How dreary would our nation be if we really were on the edge of hell today? It would be as dreary as if there were no faith, hope, or love left in our hearts. The music would fall silent; the poets would be speechless; the romance of life would dissipate. We should have no enjoyment, pleasure, or excitement left in the dark ending of our world. The eternal life of God—the one who makes all things new—would be extinguished.

Believe America Is Going to Hell?

You might as well not believe in life. You might be tempted to believe the purveyors of doom and gloom out to prove how we are guilty of manifold wickedness, to catch the nation in the act of decline, but even if they offered actual evidence of our decline, there is so much positive evidence giving the lie to their claims.

It's as if no one sees the goodness, cooperation, mutuality, commensality, friendship, empathy, good neighbor actions still unfolding daily from sea to shining sea.

The teachers who faithfully, professionally, and with great love teach our children every day in spite of fierce opposition from the warriors of the "culture war" give me hope we are not going to hell.

The people who serve around the world in our military and our first responders here at home increase my hope America is not going to hell.

The long-distance truck drivers who keep our economy humming indicate we are not going to hell.

Our best scholars, thinkers, and professors training next-generation successors accelerate my hope.

Even the boiler-plate positive TedTalks of our day remind me of how much good there is in our midst.

I am convinced the doom and gloom preachers and politicians suffer from refractive eye diseases. Their vision is blurred. They are experiencing the consequences of swallowing too many lies, conspiracy theories, and false histories of our nation.

Evangelicals fail to see that America holds the potential for a national vision premised on rights, freedoms, and democratic participation as hinted at in its founding documents. However, given that such an America was founded on imperialism and colonialism with their attendants of oppression and exploitation, its twin, Amerikkka, surfaces.[7]

Claiming "America is going to hell" against a vast preponderance of evidence to the contrary suggests historical amnesia of other eras of temporary darkness from which the nation emerged stronger. Evangelical mistrust of history and the attempt to rewrite history as a glorious Christian past seems to contradict a current rhetoric of doom and gloom. Is America a Christian nation? Or is America doomed to hell?

Robert Jeffress, perhaps unwittingly, expresses the evangelical ambivalence in his book *Twilight's Last Gleaming: Your Last Days Can Be Your Best Days*, by preaching destruction and "best days" side by side.[8] Even Jeffress is not sure as he preaches the soon return of Jesus and revels in the glory of his magnificent $125-million sanctuary in the heart of Dallas.

Sure, America has problems, complex problems, but that is no sign we are going to hell. The greatest realities in the universe are not what we are doing but what God will bring to pass with a new heaven and a new earth.

7. Holling and Moon, "20/20 in 2020?," 437.
8. Jeffress, *Twilight's Last Gleaming*, 1.

You may never have seen angels dancing in the trees. You may not believe all the miracles are literally true, but that's no proof we are going to hell. "Nobody can conceive or imagine all the wonders God has prepared for those who love. We live in the hope that the creation itself will be set free from its bondage to decay and will obtain the freedom of the glory of the children of God."[9] And that is the opposite of a nation going to hell.

The doom and gloom preachers and politicians may pile up false-cause connections, list all the alleged sins of our culture, but there is a hope the strongest people never can tear apart. The goodness, grace, and generosity of God is real. It is much more real than the false claims God is going to get us for being so bad, or that God is passing out cancer, heart attacks, or walking around the earth killing innocent people.

Going to hell? No, America is not going to hell. God lives and is on God's throne. A thousand years from now, ten times ten thousand years from now, when preachers still trot out the same old doom and gloom, there will still be so many good people doing all the good they can for all the people they can to make glad the heart of humanity.

9. Rom 8:21, paraphrase.

MAGA Followers Are Not Stupid

T HE STUPID EPIDEMIC HAS arrived. Entire Christian denominations insist there is only one way to read the Bible, and they expel
anyone daring to dissent. Politicians and the media reach for the
accusation of "stupid" out of the intractable arguments. The echoes of
"stupid" fill our social media, eating away at democratic principles of
equality, freedom, and mutual respect.

In political and religious arguments, the word *stupid* keeps popping
up as the ultimate argument against dissent.

This happens in reference to MAGA supporters believing Donald
Trump—a comfort piece of rhetorical junk food for Trump critics. A recent Salon article sums up the typical attitude: "'Too Stupid to Know Better': MAGA Eats Up Trump's Idiot President Defense."[1] Jonathan Haidt
penned an article for the *Atlantic*: "Why the Past Ten Years of American
Life Have Been Uniquely Stupid."[2]

Mark Leibovich says many of Trump's most loyal apologists are
"complete imbeciles." He calls Trump-backed candidates a collection
of "cranks, bozos and racists."[3] Joe Scarborough responding to the Representative Marjorie Taylor Greene–led effort to expunge the past impeachments of former President Donald Trump almost shouted, "It's

1. Marcotte, "Too Stupid to Know Better."
2. Haidt, "Past Ten Years."
3. Leibovich, "Tipping Point of Stupid."

just so stupid!"[4] Writing for *Jezebel*, Laura Bassett slammed Senator Josh Hawley's Juneteenth remarks as "mind-blowingly stupid."[5]

Frustrated liberals have surrendered all attempts at rational argument and gone straight to *stupid* accusations.

But guess what? There's no value in calling anyone stupid.

Stupid is a word that still jars me. My mother never allowed the word in our home. One *stupid* at the dining room table would cost you your evening meal. She thought *stupid* belonged with all the words of English profanity.

Where Has This Sudden Explosion of "Stupid" Originated?

Perhaps Donald Trump started the fad of calling people stupid. The media has compiled long lists of the people Trump has called stupid or "losers" or "mentally ill." He called Karl Rove stupid five times. *Bloomberg*'s Tim O'Brien earned the description three times, as did television host Glenn Beck. Trump has referred to Representative Maxine Waters (Democrat, California) as "low IQ," a pejorative generally reserved for her, seven times. He used the term to describe actor Robert De Niro after De Niro insulted him. He has described Don Lemon as unintelligent three times.[6]

Stupid or any of its variations seems the argument *du jour*. Like a gunslinger pulling his pistols in a crowded bar over the slightest offense, many Christians reach for *stupid* when someone dares disagree with "what the Bible says" or "what they know is the literal truth of God."

The distance between a respectful conversation and *stupid* shrinks daily. My own Facebook day would be incomplete without at least one "What kind of preacher are you?" or "Have you ever read Genesis 19?" or "You are dumb as rocks."

Attempts at reasoned argument and rational deliberation disintegrate within minutes in a single transaction with my evangelical friends. Why does this have to be our way of communicating frustration? I have spent a lifetime believing words matter, reasons matter, and rational discernment is determinative to how Americans make decisions.

4. Hall, "Joe Scarborough."
5. Bassett, "Sen. Josh Hawley."
6. Lee and Quealy, "Insulted on Twitter."

But now, in this highly oxygenated environment, reason has left town, replaced with hyperbole, untruthful, incoherent claims, and constant repetition of divisive tactics, harsh words, and violent allusions.

If liberals think the future lies in calling conservatives stupid, we miss the point that they are attracted to how Trump talks and acts.

Words like *stupid* and *idiot* shut down thought. The use of the word *stupid* in the so-called culture war really means, "Don't look for solutions." If the purpose of calling someone *stupid* is to save time by ending the debate, then it is a sure-fire time-saving device. If the opponent is stupid, then you do not need to investigate why they made such a statement, or look into their motivations, or try to understand them.

Like all "junk food," the assumption of stupidity contains no substance. Rhetorical scholar Ryan Skinnell says, "The easiest source of comfort is to believe Trump's supporters are either (a) stupid or (b) evil."[7] Both sides end up consuming rhetorical junk food that serves only as "comfort food."

The word *stupid* transfers the question from the ordinary realm of debate to a sinister, elitist, metaphysical one. To call someone stupid is a human rights violation because you are refusing to recognize your opponent as a rational creature. And that denial of rational creaturehood is at the heart of all human rights violations. It accounts for how humans are so capable of demeaning, annihilating, enslaving, and destroying one another.

Stupid or *idiot* conjures up the darkest of human DNA: dehumanization. David Livingston Smith, in *Less than Human*, explains, "Subhumans, it was believed, are beings that lack that special something that makes us human. Because of this deficit, they don't command the respect that we, the truly human beings, are obliged to grant one another. They can be enslaved, tortured or even exterminated—treated in ways in which we could not bring ourselves to treat those whom we regard as members of our own kind. This phenomenon is called dehumanization."[8]

Calling another person stupid dehumanizes them, makes them less than human. This is how the enlightened minds of our founding fathers worked as they insisted on all men being created equal and proceeded to make African Americans count as less than human.

---

7. Skinnell, "What Passes for Truth," 87.
8. Smith, *Less than Human*, 2.

Calling MAGA followers stupid doesn't convince anyone to desert Trump or face the truth. Trump's supporters are not just suckers falling for a scam. They know he is a serial liar, yet they still trust him.

Chris Christie was booed at the conservative Faith and Freedom Coalition conference in Washington, DC, after criticizing Trump. Christie reached for the "idiot" line in comments to reporters after the conference: "This guy offered me White House chief of staff and then was on a podcast yesterday saying he never trusted me. What does that make him—a liar or an idiot? It's one or the other. Because if you offered me chief of staff and you never trusted me, then you're an idiot. And if you did trust me enough to offer me chief of staff, then you're a liar."[9]

Trump has constructed a drama where his followers are under attack from a secular, atheist, evil world, and he, and he alone, can save them. He has convinced Evangelicals he can turn the world they fear into a stable world again.

"The reason that a staggering lie can pass is not only that it stabilizes an inherently unstable world by declaring it stable, but that it displays a world which we wished existed, a world in which evil was manageable, if not by us, at least by God,"[10] according to Terrence Tilley.

MAGA supporters believe Trump with the same intensity that many Evangelicals believe the earth is only a few thousand years old, that gays are an abomination to God, and that women should not be pastors. Attempt to engage anyone who believes these ideas and you will be treated to an assault of gigantic proportions. The intensity, the emotional intensity, is not evidence of stupidity.

"Liberal Attempts to 'Educate' MAGA Is Wasted Time"

What this means is that the liberal attempts to "educate" MAGA is wasted time. "Getting to know" Trump supporters is beside the point. And calling them stupid is a worthless rhetorical trick.

Progressives need a different line of attack. That begins with a different target audience. Chaim Perelman called it the universal audience. The person in your face will probably never change, but the ongoing debate among the universal audience—the collection of all rational human

9. Bahney, "Chris Christie."

10. Tilley, *Evils of Theodicy*, 247–48.

beings—will tilt in incremental ways in the direction of truth and justice. We are better served to stick with our values, our arguments. Change minds one at a time—incremental progress. God has given us all the time in the world to speak the good news. There's no rush.

Articulate the biblical, philosophical, historical realities with as much passion as possible. Repeat the arguments often. Not a bad lifetime of work.

Harris Represents the "Thorn" in Trump's Flesh: Strong, Intelligent Women

KAMALA HARRIS PRESENTS A serious challenge to Donald Trump precisely because she is a strong, intelligent woman.

Strong women always have been the "thorns" in the flesh of Trump. He can't help himself when faced with a woman with nerves of steel.

When Trump thinks he's losing control of the narrative, his instincts are to engage in racism or sexism. Speaking of Harris among world leaders, he said, "She'll be like a play toy. They look at her, and they say, 'We can't believe we got so lucky.' They're going to walk all over her."[1]

The story I am telling has a strong theme: "Democracy" has become a feminine word. Strong women are going to save democracy. As Nancy Pelosi has said, "American democracy is majestic, but it is fragile. Many of us here have witnessed its fragility firsthand, tragically. . . . And so, democracy must forever be defended from forces that wish it harm."[2]

Trump's disgusting comments about women didn't cost him significant evangelical votes and may be a tell in understanding why Evangelicals are so inept at dealing with sexual abuse and assault in their churches.

Trump has a deep emotional need to be "one up" on women and for women to be in a "one-down" position. Author Ta-Nehisi Coates says, "White supremacy has always had a perverse sexual tint."[3]

1. Concepcion, "Like a Play Toy."
2. Pelosi, "Pelosi Floor Speech."
3. Coates, "First White President."

Racism and sexism always have been twin abusers in American culture. They have left a trail of abuse, physical violence, disrespect, and pain across our land for centuries. The pain has gone deep into women.

When women finally were making actual gains, along came Trump wearing white maleness like an ancestral talisman. He "cracked the glowing amulet," Coates says, "releasing its eldritch energies,"[4] and setting back women's rights by more than fifty years.

Trump is a male-centered primate who feels superior to women.

Trump Has a Long Record as a Misogynist

Trump has a rap sheet longer than a drug dealer when it comes to verbal attacks on women.

Trump has called women "horseface," "dog," and "big fat pig." In particular, he leaps at every opportunity to call Black women "racist," "nasty," stupid, "low-IQ," "monsters," or "unqualified."

Among illustrations of his misogyny:

+ He declared, "Rosie O'Donnell is disgusting—both inside and out. If you take a look at her, she's a slob. How does she even get on television? If I were running *The View*, I'd fire Rosie. I'd look her right in that fat, ugly face of hers and say, 'Rosie, you're fired.' We're all a little chubby, but Rosie's just worse than most of us."[5]

+ He told *Celebrity Apprentice* contestant and former Playboy Playmate Brande Roderick, "It must be a pretty picture. You dropping to your knees."[6]

+ He told *Esquire*, "You know, it doesn't really matter what [the media] write as long as you've got a young and beautiful piece of ass."[7]

+ He speculated that he could've had sex with Princess Diana if he'd wanted to before her death, called avoiding STDs from casual sex his "personal Vietnam," assigned each actor on *Desperate Housewives* an attractiveness score from one to ten (on Nicollette Sheridan: "A person who is very flat-chested is very hard to be a 10").[8]

4. Coates, "First White President."
5. Stack, "Rosie O'Donnell."
6. Trump, cited in Charlton, "Married Donald Trump."
7. Rappeport, "Trail of Comments."
8. Matthews, "Every Horrible Thing."

Strong Women Are a Thorn in Trump's Flesh

Jessica Bennett of the *New York Times* did a roll call of Trump's "thorns in the flesh": "Letitia James. Fani Willis. E. Jean Carroll and her lawyer, Roberta Kaplan. And, of course, Stormy Daniels. The five women who are living rent-free in Mr. Trump's mind these days."[9] Bennett added, "Depending on how you count them, 19 or 26 or 67 women have accused Mr. Trump of sexual misconduct. Women who have said he 'squeezed my butt,' 'eyed me like a piece of meat,' 'stuck his hand up my skirt,' 'thrust his genitals,' 'forced his tongue in my mouth,' was 'rummaging around my vagina,' and so on."[10]

Willis is the prosecutor in Trump's election subversion case in Fulton County, Georgia. James is the New York attorney general. In that case, Donald Trump, his adult sons, and former executives were ordered to pay more than $450 million they fraudulently and illegally obtained.

Carroll and her attorney, Kaplan, defeated Trump twice in civil lawsuits. Trump has been ordered to pay almost ninety million dollars to Carroll.

Politically, the biggest thorn in Trump's flesh has been Nancy Pelosi. Trump enjoys comparing himself to Jesus, especially his persecution. Well, Pelosi, more than any other person, has pushed down on Trump's head "a crown of thorns." She is the thorniest, toughest opponent Trump ever has faced.

Pelosi attacks Trump's sensitive male persona. She goads him for lacking courage to face her personally or to come to Congress to confront her.

After a contentious White House meeting with Trump, Pelosi said she was "trying to be the mom in the room." She continued, "It's like a manhood thing for him. As if manhood could ever be associated with him."[11]

While the male members of the Republican Party are deathly afraid of Trump and MAGA, Pelosi remains unimpressed and not afraid at all. Representative Scott Peters put it best: "She was Donald Trump's biggest problem."[12] Pelosi majors in "butt-kicking" not "ring-kissing."

---

9. Bennett, "Stormy Daniels."
10. Bennett, "Strange Sorority."
11. Montoya-Galvez, "Pelosi Questions."
12. Politi and Weaver, "Trump's Biggest Problem."

How Does Trump Get Away with It?

Trump gets away with his treatment of women because his base consists of white males riddled with resentment.

Trump's largest MAGA group, the Southern Baptist Convention, has its own "woman problem." The SBC prohibits women from serving as pastors in its churches. It insists women are to be "submissive" to their husbands. It struggles to create a consistent polity for dealing with sexual abuse among pastors.

SBC men hide their authority with biblical appeals and the word "complementarian." Yet even in the culture of honeysuckle, New International Bibles, pompous authoritarian pastors, and the ubiquitous demands for submission, one can only smile when strong, independent, intelligent women are seen "bossing" their husbands, making sure churches remain viable, and providing half or more of a family's income.

Trump and his Southern Baptist macho men can run, hide, and deny, but where can they go from the presence of strong, intelligent women?

Biblical Accounts of Strong Women

In the same Bible where male Southern Baptists oligarchs find defense for "lording it over women," there are an array of strong women, sometimes with questionable moral character, influencing events.

- ◆ There's Rahab, the Jericho prostitute, who saved the spies of Israel and was the first person within the bounds of the promised land to express faith in Israel's God.
- ◆ There's Delilah, who tricked Samson into revealing the secret of his great strength. The Philistines cut his hair and imprisoned him.
- ◆ There's Jael, who took a tent peg and a hammer in her hands and went softly to Sisera, the Canaanite general, and drove the peg into his temple until it went down into the ground—he was lying fast asleep from weariness—and he died.
- ◆ There's Naomi and Ruth, who ganged up to find a husband for Ruth.
- ◆ There's Bathsheba, wife of Uriah, who was sexually assaulted by King David. When the king was old, Bathsheba deceived the king, with the help of the court preacher, Nathan, and convinced him to declare her son, Solomon, king of Israel.

- ◆ There's Esther, outsmarting Haman to save the Jews from genocide.

There's no shortage of strong, intelligent women in the Bible changing the course of history.

Even Jesus created a distraction when he seemingly referred to a foreign woman as a dog. She responded with one of the greatest comebacks of all time: "Yes, Lord, yet even the dogs eat the crumbs that fall from their masters' table."[13] As Ellen Davis points out, "Jesus submits to be instructed on no small point of holiness by a woman whom Matthew pointedly designates a 'Canaanite.'"[14]

It is hard to be more patriarchal than the Bible, but even there, the strong women stand out.

A Story of Strong, Smart Women from History

Close to the medieval town of Weinsberg in Southern Germany stand the ruins of a medieval castle. This once-imposing fortress was the site of a lengthy siege in the twelfth century, which sparked a popular local legend. Conrad of Hohenstaufen permitted the women of the castle to leave unhindered, together with whatever they could carry on their backs.

The clever women of Weinsberg defied him by leaving behind their provisions and walking from the castle with the men on their backs.

Harris, a strong, independent, smart woman, now carries the hopes and dreams of democracy on her back. She shares the load with like-minded women everywhere. Breathing fresh air into the almost morgue-like campaign between two "old geezers," Harris has injected euphoria.

There is evidence Trump struggles to decide how best to attack Harris. He told a recent rally crowd he wouldn't be nice. "She's one of the worst prosecutors in history," he lamented.[15]

Trump lives in his own self-constructed world where he "lords" it over everyone, and women are at his disposal. He believes he is a ladies' man. He has said, "I will be phenomenal to the women."[16]

During his first run for president, Trump insisted he would be the best for women and their health issues. Of course, that was before he

13. Matt 15:27.
14. Davis and Hays, *Art of Reading Scripture*, 177.
15. Politi and Weaver, "'Trump's Biggest Problem.'"
16. Kaplan, "I Will Be Phenomenal."

appointed two conservative Supreme Court justices who moved quickly to spearhead the overthrow of Roe v. Wade.

No Grace Sufficient for Trump's Misogyny

After the apostle Paul prayed three times for the removal of his thorn, God gave him the answer of "grace sufficient." Trump, not a man of prayer, has no way of avoiding the thorns in his flesh.

Betul Eksi and Elizabeth A. Wood, in "Right-Wing Populism as Gendered Performance: Janus-Faced Masculinity in the Leadership of Vladimir Putin and Recep T. Erdogan," outline three keys to understanding authoritarian male leaders: populist masculine performances, nativism that rejects the masculinity of others, and direct paternal rule, as in "I am the only one who can save you."[17]

Eksi's and Wood's "Janus"[18] metaphor reveals the Trump face. The bad boy wins approval from the cult, and then the good father protects the nation.

The ostentatious masculine posturing that has served Trump so well will come crumbling down around him. The male monster has clay feet.

Trump's masculine image is his entire game. He has bet everything on the voters falling for his bad boy but good father image. He deliberately chose this image because it is his most natural persona.

As Trump keeps "being Trump," keeps running on the same tired cliches, slogans, threats, and insults from his first term, more voters will see him for what he is—a scared, insecure, old man unable to deal with the thorn in his flesh, Kamala Harris.

17. Eksi and Wood, "Right-Wing Populism," 733.
18. Eksi and Wood, "Right-Wing Populism," 737.

It's Time to Become American Nazi Hunters

THERE ARE NAZIS IN our midst. Not just Nazi flag–carrying, swastika-wearing, swashbuckling Nazi-saluting members of American neo-Nazi groups, but ordinary Americans who will swear they are not Nazis. It's now obvious that MAGA has Nazi leanings.

Psychologist Keith Payne, in *Good Reasonable People: The Psychology Behind America's Dangerous Divide*, argues most Americans consider themselves "good, reasonable people." That would include the Americans who stormed the US Capitol on January 6, 2021, the Americans who engaged in vandalism in our cities, the Americans who viciously attacked and threatened an Episcopal bishop over a sermon, the Americans who call one another every name in the English language on social media, and the Americans who entertain Nazi ideas.

As the eightieth anniversary of the liberation of Auschwitz was commemorated January 27, the far right was soaring all over the world. Perhaps historical ignorance plays a role in our forgetting what must never be forgotten. Evidence: a survey by the Conference on Jewish Material Claims Against Germany found among one thousand Americans questioned, almost half (48 percent), could not name a single concentration camp.[1]

Meanwhile, the global right-wing surge includes a neo-Nazi movement in Germany. No nation has worked harder to reckon with its history than Germany. Germans have attempted to pull out by the roots the best known version of fascism in history—the Nazis.

Yet in the country where making a Nazi salute is a crime, the far-right neo-Nazi party, the Alternative for Deutschland, has become the

---

1. *Jewish Chronicle*, "Nazi Death Camp."

second largest political group with 20 percent support among Germans.[2] If Nazism can be reborn in Germany, then obviously it has a field white unto harvest in America.

America has reproduced 1932 Germany. Fascism is a populist, re- actionary spirit poised for dominance. The immigrant crisis, the rise of white supremacists, white male reactions to a Black man being in the White House for eight years, economic uncertainty, and a feeling the sys- tem is rigged against white people make fertile soil for fascism. MAGA evangelical frustration with a powerful civic morality that produced liberal rights for women, gays, lesbians, transgender people, and immi- grants has driven their faith group in the direction of authoritarianism. They are more concerned with preserving a white-centered tradition than protecting democracy.

The new Evangelicalism was born in the 1980s out of a racist, seg- regationist fervor, and the current manifestation has taken on even more fascist ideas.

Two unrelated social media moments focused my attention on the possibility of Nazis in the garden of democracy.

Refusing to Denounce Nazism

First, here's a post that shows the weird reasoning behind the old saying, "The enemy of my enemy is my friend."

On X, Mike Cosper, senior director of *Christianity Today* media, addresses a MAGA tweet refusing to denounce Nazis: "This is amazing. Won't denounce Nazis because denouncement itself is left coded. No regrets on sharing the White Boy Summer video (which contains lit- eral Third Reich propaganda and appears to celebrate famous American Neo-Nazis side-by-side with images from their churches) because there's no reason to explain Zoomer humor and memes to out of touch Boom- ers. Likens not alienating Nazis in their church to not alienating Flat Earthers, which ought to win an Olympic medal for the stupidest moral equivalence in an age of many, many stupid moral equivalences. What's wild to me is that these men would break fellowship with a professed Christian who wanted to be part of Revoice faster than you can blink. But someone who would justify the slaughter of 11 million people in service of ethnonationalist purity? All the patience and grace in the world."[3]

2. Duggal, "Germany's Far-Right."
3. Cosper, "This is amazing."

As is typical of the social media platform X, the backlash against Cosper was swift and vicious.

Elon Musk's Nazi Salute

Second, there's Elon Musk's Nazi salute. There was no mistaking the gesture from Musk at Donald Trump's inaugural festivities. A ham-handed Nazi salute to warm the hearts of Neo-Nazis around the world was on full display. Speaking during the inaugural parade inside Capitol One Arena in Washington, DC, on January 20, Musk gave two Nazi salutes and said, "My heart goes out to you."[4]

We all saw it! And the excuses and rationalizations by Musk and MAGA never will change what we saw—a "Heil Hitler" salute. Musk pushes us into the darkness with a pair of Nazi salutes. Across the eighty-eight years since 1937, there is no mistaking the gesture. Then and now it strikes fear into our hearts.

Musk, responding to criticism of his Nazi-like salute, said of his critics, "Frankly, they need better dirty tricks. The 'everyone is Hitler attack is too tired.'"[5]

Only in Musk's mind can this be seen as a rational explanation. What about the salute?

Bill Gates, a sane billionaire, put it exactly right: "'You want to promote the right wing but say Nigel Farage is not right wing enough. . . . I mean, this is insane shit. You are for the AfD [in Germany].' Is he embarrassed that a billionaire techie has gone rogue? 'We can all overreach. . . . If someone is super-smart, and he is, they should think how they can help out. But this is populist stirring.'"[6]

Even if there was a tendency to give Musk a break, his additional actions made this impossible. Strike one: Musk posted a series of jokes using names connected with the Holocaust. Strike two: he gave a Nazi salute. Strike three: he spoke by video to the neo-Nazi party in Germany, the AfD, and told the Germans to get over their guilt.

"Something I think that is just very important is that people take pride in Germany and being German. This is very important," Musk said.

---

4. Warzel, "Did He Actually Do That?"
5. Crane, "Elon Musk."
6. Thomson, "Bill Gates"; ellipses and brackets in original.

"It's, you know, it's OK to be proud to be German. This is a very important principle."[7]

Heil Hitler!

If we agree we should oppose any suggestion of Nazi ideology with the same fervor as rejecting the devil, then there is no room for Nazi salutes, ideas, or principles in our democracy.

Nazi Hunters

The Amazon television series *Hunters* portrays a group of Nazi hunters tracking down the thousands of former Nazis who infiltrated the United States after World War II. A Nazi hunter is an individual who tracks down and gathers information on alleged former Nazis, or SS members, and Nazi collaborators who were involved in the Holocaust.

I am a Nazi hunter, not in the historical sense but in the rhetorical and political sense of identifying Nazi sympathizers or appeasers. This is my purpose: finding the evidence, presenting it in a rational fashion, and deciding if a full alarm should sound.

Kenneth Burke in 1939 urged writers "to find all available ways of making the Hitlerite distortions of religion apparent, in order that politicians of his kind in America be unable to perform a similar swindle."[8]

This is not a hunt for full-fledged Nazis. The Southern Poverty Law Center has identified at least ninety-two neo-Nazi groups in the United States.[9] Frankly, Franklin Graham frightens me more than a group of bald, swastika-sashed, middle-aged white Americans on motorcycles. Most Americans are not members of any of these groups. My hunt is more of an epistemological search for Nazi sympathizers and appeasers.

What are we hunting? Fascism. Fascism is a populist political philosophy, movement, or regime that exalts nation and often race above the individual, that is associated with a centralized autocratic government headed by a dictatorial leader, and that is characterized by severe economic and social regimentation and by forcible suppression of opposition.

7. NBC News, "German Crowd."
8. Burke, "Rhetoric of Hitler's 'Battle,'" 219.
9. Southern Poverty Law Center, "Hate Map."

Three of the major characteristics of the MAGA movement are nativism, racism, and authoritarianism. At the core of fascism is loyalty to tribe, ethnic identity, religion, tradition, or, in a word, nation. Unconditional loyalty, no dissension in the ranks, and total conformity among MAGA Evangelicals and Republicans sounds so fascist.

Add the fog of white superiority and you have the trappings of a new Nazi movement. Evangelicals deny the existence of racism, but they haven't stopped being racists. They have moved the target of their racism from Blacks to brown people—immigrants.

After all, when Hitler came to power, most Germans were not members of the Nazi Party. Historians suggest between 12 percent and 35 percent of adult Germans were formally members of the Nazi Party or supporters of the Nazis.[10]

Hitler didn't have to persuade everyone; he only had to convince enough people to allow him to act on his hardcore beliefs. Many Germans already believed much of what Hitler said before Hitler made his first speech. Patricia Roberts-Miller, retired professor of rhetoric and author of a major work on demagoguery, says, "He wasn't some kind of all-powerful magical rhetor who waved a word-wand and transformed good people into bad."[11]

We now know people should have taken the threat of Hitler more seriously than they did long before they did. Where are our Winston Churchills? Early and often Churchill blasted the warnings, "We are in the presence of a disaster of the first magnitude. . . . Do not suppose that this is the end. This is only the beginning of the reckoning. This is only the first foretaste of a bitter cup which will be proffered to us year by year unless by a supreme recovery of moral health and martial vigor, we arise again and take our stand for freedom."[12]

Authoritarianism the Root of Nazism

Among us today, Cornel West is Churchillian in his warnings about the dogma of authoritarianism.

---

10. Roberts-Miller, "Rhetoric and Hitler."
11. Roberts-Miller, "Rhetoric and Hitler."
12. Churchill, "Munich Agreement."

"This dogma is rooted in our understandable paranoia toward potential terrorists, our traditional fear of too many liberties, and our deep distrust of one another," he has said.[13]

It is also a reaction to the influence of liberals in making such sweeping changes to America that have caused Evangelicals to believe the country has been taken away from them.

When safety trumps liberty, when security usurps compassion, we have authoritarianism rooted in paranoia. When Evangelicals desert faith for Christian nationalism, they are only a step away from authoritarianism. If they insist on supporting a serial liar as their supreme leader, they are on the slippery slope toward fascism. Evangelical emotional subjectivism and populism have provided the foundation for a new fascist movement.

The attraction of authoritarianism, the *genus* of Nazism, arises from an extreme prejudice against liberals. MAGA evangelical hatred of liberalism, for example, blinds them to the possibility of a turn toward Nazism.

The Appeal of Nazism

What is the appeal of Nazism? Hitler's rise to power depended upon many Germans already thinking like Hitler. He convinced Germans they were the real victims. The German people had been mistreated. Miller-Roberts offers a helpful critique:

> What he said was: You're in a bad situation; it can't be your fault. You're a German, so it can't be Germany's fault. It's the liberals. Who are Jews. And Bolsheviks. And international financiers. All true Germans agree. Our government sucks because it isn't giving you the things you know you deserve, and it isn't dominating every other country, and God wants us to be the best, and democracy involves letting other people argue and they're all wrong and so it's a waste of time because the true course of action is obvious to every reasonable person and so elect someone who cares about people like you. And who will insist that Germany is the best.[14]

She continues, "Politicians who say it's complicated are just trying to line their own pockets. Democratic deliberation is a waste of time—just hand over all the power to a guy who can get things done. And that's me."[15]

13. West, *Democracy Matters*, 6.
14. Miller-Roberts, "Rhetoric and Hitler."
15. Miller-Roberts, "Rhetoric and Hitler."

The Nazis made huge promises: a strong country, military strength, increased territory, greater wealth. They delivered with territorial aggression and antidemocratic measures. They disliked voting, banned other political parties, and realigned the bureaucracy with the Nazi Party. People were so interested in a strong country, they did not mind what shape that strength would take.

The Nazis offered unity. They promised a country not overrun by individualism, and they built it on conformity. What they did not like, they banned. Objectionable books, films, newspapers, and opinions were silenced or destroyed. People who did not align were quieted or eliminated. The Nazis opposed liberty in every respect. They dissolved the boundary between public and private life.

Unity required the elimination of internal enemies. People were willing to put up with authoritarian rule to be rid of political and cultural differences. But the list of internal enemies is always capable of expanding and must expand if you are attempting to sustain power with fear-based rhetoric and totalitarian measures.

The Nazis claimed to be the party of traditional values. They opposed the new and edgy culture of the Weimar Republic with its changing gender roles, modern art, and imported nontraditional music. The Nazis were pronatalist and anti-abortion; they created government policies to encourage women to stay home with their families. The MAGA evangelical culture war script (Project 2025) reads like the Nazi culture war script.

In 1937, Pope Pius XI warned against the Third Reich in his papal encyclical *Mit Brennender Sorge* ("With Burning Anxiety"): "Whoever exalts race, or the people, or the state, or a particular form of state, or the depositories of power, or any other fundamental value of the human community—however necessary and honorable be their function in worldly things—whoever raises these notions above their standard value and divinizes them to an idolatrous level, distorts and perverts an order of the world planned and created by God; he is far from the true faith in God and from the concept of life which that faith upholds."[16]

Imagine Pope Pius XI at a Turning Point USA gathering and telling the assembled Christian nationalists, "None but superficial minds could stumble into concepts of a national God, of a national religion, or attempt to lock within the frontiers of a single people, within the narrow limits of

16. Pius XI, *Mit Brennender Sorge*, §8.

a single race, God, the Creator of the universe, King and Legislator of all nations before whose immensity they are 'as a drop of a bucket.'"[17]

Evangelicals are in no mood for advice from a pope, an Episcopal bishop, or any liberal pastor. They have sold out to "We are right" and "Might makes right."

In an authoritarian culture, the in-group has rights, but no one else does. Everyone else should be grateful they are not more oppressed than they already are. When Evangelicals are provoked, they engage in outrageous criticism, but it always is the fault of the "provoker."

Where's Churchill Today?

I can't imagine an evangelical preacher with the courage of Churchill. I can make a list of the evangelical preachers willing to play the role of Neville Chamberlain and Joseph Kennedy—famous appeasers of Hitler—Robert Jeffress and Franklin Graham among them.

Yes, I expect disbelief from MAGA Evangelicals.

There will be a strong sense of disbelief of the idea of Nazis in our midst. In *Our Nazi: An American Suburb's Encounter with Evil* by Michael Soffer, we have the story of Reinhold Kulle. He was discovered to be a former Nazi. And not just any Nazi but a member of the Waffen SS's infamous Death's Head Division.

Yet he believed he had done nothing wrong. He received support from churches and American conservatives. How long were you expected to bear responsibility for actions committed forty years earlier? Weren't Christians required to forgive in such cases? What was the point of spending public resources on hounding people now in their sixties out of the country?

No matter how ordinary, normal, or even Christian someone appears, if there are Nazi ideas, actions, and beliefs, this person is not one of us.

Our anti-Nazi battle remains clear: any hint of Nazi ideology must be exposed, refuted, and dismissed. And if a group of neo-Nazis shows up in your neighborhood brandishing swastikas, Nazi flags, and giving Nazi salutes, protest peacefully and nonviolently, but above all, protest their heinous ideology.

---

17. Pius XI, *Mit Brennender Sorge*, §11.

Now the US House Wants to
Censor a Preacher?

W HEN POLITICIANS ACT LIKE preachers, we get members of the House of Representatives falling over themselves to sponsor House Resolution 59 condemning Bishop Mariann Budde, the Episcopal bishop of Washington, DC.

Imagine the House of Representatives taking time away from its current agenda on taxes, tariffs, immigration, birthright citizenship, and cutting food stamps to attack a bishop's sermon. This is absurd.

As is well-known by now, Budde preached the sermon Tuesday at the traditional inaugural prayer service with President Donald Trump and Vice President J. D. Vance in attendance. As I watched the service, I knew it would not go well because our nation's two most powerful leaders were laughing and rolling their eyes during the reading of the Scripture.

After the service, Budde was assaulted by a crescendo of criticism led by Trump with his usual trope calling her "nasty." A choir of Republican leaders and MAGA Evangelicals took up the song to blast the bishop.

All the bloviating reached the offices of the US House of Representatives, where a group of politicians pretending to have religious knowledge, acting in complete contradiction of the First Amendment to the Constitution, dared to offer what amounts to censorship of a clergyperson.

Even if this resolution were to pass, it is not worth "a bucket of warm spit." But it shows the danger of having half-ass politicians acting like half-ass preachers.

House Resolution 59 is sponsored by Representative Josh Brecheen of Oklahoma with twenty-one cosponsors. The full title of the bill introduced in the House (it is hard to imagine reading this all the way through without bursting into laughter): "Expressing the sense of the House of Representatives that the sermon given by the Right Reverend Mariann Edgar Budde at the National Prayer Service on January 21 at the National Cathedral was a display of political activism and condemning its distorted message."[1]

When the response to a sermon is outrage and a desire to censor takes root, there is a strong possibility truth has been spoken but rejected.

As to the sermon being an example of political activism and a distorted message, half these politicians are up to their steeples in misinformation, misinterpretation, and plain bad manners.

For decades, conservatives have insisted issues of homosexuality are biblical in nature. Now, when an Episcopal bishop pleads for mercy for gays, lesbians, and transgender people, conservatives see that as "political activism." Not what they've been doing, of course, only what someone on the other side does.

And the bishop carried on the clear biblical tradition of appealing for compassion for immigrants and refugees—something that once was mainstream Christian belief but has been hijacked by the MAGA mind meld.

Trump and his allies at the National Cathedral want to remake the Bible in their political image rather than be challenged by the truth of Scripture.

As Episcopal priest and scholar Ellen F. Davis reminds, "Using the text to confirm our presuppositions is sinful; it is an act of resistance against God's fresh speaking to us, an effective denial that the Bible is the word of the living God."[2]

Trump and his allies in the House do not understand there's more to Christianity than the evangelical base that supports them.

There always has been a more powerful voice in Christianity than the fundamentalist-to-evangelical voice. These House members seem utterly ignorant of the powerful tradition of the social gospel in American Christianity. They may not know that Evangelicals, in the late nineteenth century, were deeply involved in support of the right of women to vote, the organization of unions, and care for the poor. Evangelicals were for the social gospel before they were against it.

1. H.R. 59, 119th Cong. (2025–2026).
2. Davis and Hays, *Art of Reading Scripture*, 16.

Somehow, MAGA politicians and preachers have decided Budde's sermon at Washington National Cathedral is the religious version of the shoot-out at the O. K. Corral. As the good guys, they came out guns blazing. They are bullying someone they think is an easy target.

But this time they picked on the wrong female bishop. She has reinforcements, a progressive church awakening to the dangers evangelical bullying holds for America. United Methodist Bishop William Willimon said that "Budde's plea for mercy was 'particularly moving.' 'There's no instance in the life, work, teachings of Jesus where mercy ever takes a backseat to anything else. . . . Not only is Jesus merciful, he commands his followers to be merciful. Even to those who are our enemies and those who wrong us, he ordered mercy,' he added."[3]

Willimon struck a nerve: Trump is "a president that's shown great mercy for convicted criminals who attacked the government in his name and yet is so stunningly unmerciful with these vulnerable immigrants and others."[4]

Reverend Paul Brandeis Raushenbush, president and CEO of Interfaith Alliance and an ordained Baptist minister, said that as he watched Budde deliver her sermon, he saw how "deeply she was drawing on her spiritual calling to say what she knew the Gospel was inspiring her to say." Raushenbush said that Budde was "acting as a pastor" to Trump in that moment. She was "giving spiritual direction to someone in her congregation who happened to be the president of the United States." "You could see that Trump was unused to anyone, much less a Christian leader, speaking to him in any way that wasn't simply delivering praise," he said, later adding, "In the kindest way, she was offering him a moment to reflect and even repent. The fact that his heart was too hardened to hear it is on him—not her."[5]

Here are a few of Bishop Budde's "offending" words: "In his Sermon on the Mount, Jesus of Nazareth exhorts us to love not only our neighbors but to love our enemies and to pray for those who persecute us, to be merciful as our God is merciful, to forgive others as God forgives us. And Jesus went out of his way to welcome those whom his society deemed as outcasts."[6]

3. Richards, "Pastor's Powerful Plea."
4. Richards, "Pastor's Powerful Plea."
5. Richards, "Pastor's Powerful Plea."
6. Budde, "Inauguration Prayer Service."

The X (formerly Twitter) world filled with venomous chatter from evangelical leaders. Denny Burke: "Be warned. This is not John the Baptist confronting Herod. This is a hidden reef in the church's love feast (Jude 12)."[7] Tony Perkins: "What we heard today was not a prophetic voice from the church, but rather pathetic."[8] Reverend Dr. Robert Jeffress: "Attended national prayer service today at the Washington National Cathedral during which Bishop Mariann Edgar Budde insulted rather than encouraged our great president @realDonaldTrump. There was palpable disgust in the audience with her words."[9]

That's Not Bible?

Far-right evangelist Lance Wallnau thought there should have been preaching by Paula White. This is the same loony tune who claimed angels were being dispatched from Africa and South America to save the election for Trump in 2020. The mind seizes at the idea of Paula White screeching in the National Cathedral and speaking in tongues.

House Speaker Mike Johnson also got his dander up: "Bishop Budde hijacked the National Prayer Service to promote her radical ideology. This was an opportunity to unify the country in prayer, but she used it to sow division. Even worse, she's continued her political crusade in media interviews. Shameful."[10]

Johnson somehow missed the twenty-five times Bishop Budde called for unity. She set the tone for her homily in the introduction: "As a country, we have gathered this morning to pray for unity as a people and a nation, not for agreement, political or otherwise, but for the kind of unity that fosters community across diversity and division, a unity that serves the common good."[11]

Johnson's call for unity smacks of hypocrisy.

After ten years of hateful, divisive language, harsh judgments, violent imagery, and demonizing progressives as servants of Satan, on what

7. Burke, "The preacher admonishing."

8. Perkins, "Cause of America's decline."

9. Jeffress, "Attended national prayer service"; for other comments, see Fea, "Demonic 'Priestess.'"

10. Chapman, "You're a Lapdog."

11. Budde, "Inauguration Prayer Service."

basis do they now want unity? I am convinced Evangelicals mean "conformity" when they use the term "unity."

And now they seem willing to flout the Constitution itself to exact their revenge. This is dangerous territory.

Representative Mike Collins (Republican, Georgia) shared a clip of the sermon on X and wrote, "The person giving this sermon should be added to the deportation list."[12]

That reminded me of Baptist fundamentalist J. Frank Norris of Fort Worth, Texas, in the 1920s claiming the government should herd Roman Catholic cardinals onto ships filled with bombs and send them out to sea to be blown up.

These self-proclaimed spokespersons of God, who act as if they have just returned from a one-on-one meeting with God on Sinai, have made fools of themselves. The accusations they fire at the bishop are unsophisticated in logic and pompous in their certainty.

The real problem here is that Budde's Bible-based sermon was a direct assault on the entire Age of Trump. She rightly proclaimed unity is only possible if we honor human dignity, if we embrace honesty, and if we model humility.

Without calling him out by name, her appeal to honor human dignity clashes with Trump's assault on almost everyone not kowtowing to his will. Her Bible message attacked his constant habit of lying. Her gospel appeal for humility smashed Trump's bragging, boasting, superhero, television star image.

Budde Preached the Gospel, and Trump Is Not a Gospel Man

The bishop spoke truth to power. The biblical models for this kind of preaching range from Moses preaching to Pharaoh, Nathan condemning David for his abuse of Bathsheba, Amos rebuking King Jeroboam, John the Baptist insisting Herod was wrong to take his brother's wife, and Saint Paul preaching to Agrippa.

12. Collins, "The person giving this sermon."

We Also Have Precedence for Such Prophetic Preaching in America

On April 4, 1967, Martin Luther King Jr. preached perhaps the greatest sermon of his life: "Beyond Vietnam: A Time to Break Silence." The sermon garnered almost universal condemnation with 168 daily newspapers castigating the great civil rights preacher for calling upon President Lyndon Johnson to have compassion on the children of Vietnam. America then was too racist, nativist, and hateful to accept the sermon.

Apparently, not much has changed. America still struggles with racism, nativism, and hatefulness.

There are more preachers like Budde than anyone knows. They preach faithful gospel sermons in obscurity and anonymity every Sunday. They carry on the prophetic tradition. Our nation's pulpits, universities, and seminaries are filled with faithful biblical scholars, theologians, ethics professors, historians, philosophers, preachers, and priests.

According to the law of our land, they are allowed to preach and teach according to the dictates of their conscience without government censorship, which is what these House members want to apply.

Budde deserves an "amen" rather than outbursts of acrimony leveled at her by preachers and politicians unworthy to carry her shepherd's crook in a liturgical processional. I hope every preacher with an ounce of courage references Bishop's Budde's plea for mercy this Sunday from the pulpit.

Live by the Mouth, Die by the Mouth

T HERE'S NO DISPUTING DONALD Trump is the all-time champion mouth.

He used his mouth to get elected president of the United States. Now, his mouth has been the primary culprit in a New York jury finding him liable for battery and defamation in the Jean Carroll case.

We are tempted to say, "The mouth giveth and the mouth taketh away."

While Jesus said, "He who lives by the sword dies by the sword,"[1] we also suggest that he who lives by the mouth may die by the mouth.

Consider some other biblical wisdom about the mouth:

- Psalm 34:13—"Keep your tongue from evil and your lips from speaking deceit."

- Matthew 12:36—"I tell you, on the day of judgment you will have to give an account for every careless word you utter."

- Proverbs 15:4—"A gentle tongue is a tree of life, but perverseness in it breaks the spirit."

- James 1:26—"If any think they are religious and do not bridle their tongues but deceive their hearts, their religion is worthless."

- Proverbs 18:21—"Death and life are in the power of the tongue, and those who love it will eat its fruits."

- James 3:6—"And the tongue is a fire. The tongue is placed among our members as a world of iniquity; it stains the whole body, sets on fire the cycle of life, and is itself set on fire by hell."

1. Matt 26:52.

Trump followers love his mouth. He makes nicknaming and name-calling into a nouveau art form. Provoked by Trump, name-calling spread like wildfire among other candidates. The attacks are personal, nasty, and childish.

For example, former Florida Governor Jeb Bush accused Trump of being "the chaos candidate." Following up while campaigning in New Hampshire, Bush called Trump a "jerk." In the debate of January 14, 2016, US Senator Ted Cruz attacked Trump's "New York values," and Trump replied that Cruz may not be a "natural-born citizen." Later Trump claimed Cruz's father was involved in the assassination of President John F. Kennedy. When US Senator Marco Rubio stooped to genital jokes about Trump, Trump responded by branding Rubio, who is short of stature, as "little Marco."[2]

Rhetorical scholar Craig R. Smith labeled Trump's "mouth" as bar talk. He said, "By 'bar talk,' I mean that Trump said things from his political pulpit that one would normally only hear after a few drinks in the privacy of an underlit bar."[3]

Trump claimed undocumented immigrants were "bringing drugs" and "crime" into the country and that some were "rapists." He called for a wall on the Mexican border that he would force Mexico to fund. Trump said he would prohibit Muslims from immigrating to America. He would bomb ISIS even if that meant killing civilians. When Trump canceled a rally at University of Illinois Chicago on March 11, 2016, demonstrators clashed with his supporters. Trump told supporters to "knock the crap out of" would-be hecklers at a campaign rally in Cedar Rapids, Iowa. "If you see somebody with a tomato, knock the crap out of them," Trump said, referencing another incident with a protestor.[4]

In his Harrisburg, Pennsylvania, rally Trump paused to watch a protester being removed: "That's right, get him out of here, get him out."[5]

He sounded tough, and his followers reveled in what they called "telling it like it is." His habit of nicknaming has become an obsession with his supporters. In his presidential campaigns, he uses verbal combat skills to the maximum. He referred to Jeb Bush as a "low-energy" candidate and labeled Ben Carson "pathological." Ted Cruz was "lyin' Ted"

2. Smith, "Rhetorical Re-Invention," 54.
3. Smith, "Rhetorical Re-Invention," 52.
4. White, "Trump Tells Crowd."
5. Miles, "Trump Pennsylvania Rally."

and a "basket case." He labeled Hillary Clinton as "crooked Hillary." Then there's "Sleepy Creepy Joe" and "Crazy Bernie."[6]

Sparing no one, Trump mocked, baited, demeaned, and cursed his way to the White House. He mockingly imitated a handicapped reporter during the 2016 campaign.

A rhetorical marker of racism in Trump's discourse is the way he refers to minorities. He calls them "the Blacks," "the Hispanics," "the Mexicans," and "the Muslims." When a judge of Hispanic descent was put in charge of the Trump University fraud case, Trump said the judge could not be objective because he was "Mexican." The judge was born in Indiana.[7]

Trump went on to claim a Muslim judge could not be objective if ruling on his case. He told US Representatives Alexandria Ocasio-Cortez of New York, Ilhan Omar of Minnesota, Rashida Tlaib of Michigan, and Ayanna S. Pressley of Massachusetts to "go back to their own countries."[8]

No one can claim the title of the nation's top mouth without a steady diet of bragging. Trump regularly claims to be a hugely successful businessman and negotiator. He regularly claims he has done more for gays or women than he has.

The ticker tape of words flowing from Trump's mouth are supported by his facial expressions. Rhetorical scholar Donovan Schaefer points out, "The visual rhetoric of Trump's body—'controlling, coercive and conceited, a combination of traits that embody white privilege and hypermasculinity'—is a necessary augmentation to the Trump script. It consolidates his status as the humiliator in chief."[9]

His people can't get enough of Trump's mouth. Twenty-four million people watched the first Republican debate in 2016. His numbers were off the charts. The media went into a frenzy of attacking Trump and secretly loving the ratings he drew and the profits they were depositing.

Trump's mouth and mannerisms reflect the image of a bully, a big-mouth, and a braggart. And now, his mouth has failed him. A New York jury has found him liable for battery and defamation and awarded five million dollars in damages.

6. Smith, "Rhetorical Re-Invention," 54.

7. Smith, "Rhetorical Re-Invention," 54.

8. Rogers and Fandos, "Trump Tells Congresswomen."

9. Schaefer, "Whiteness and Civilization," 17.

Proverbs 10:14 says, "The mouth of a fool brings ruin near." And the wise woman of Proverbs advises: "To watch over mouth and tongue is to keep out of trouble."[10]

Don't be tempted to believe the mouth has been silenced. Trump will roar even more vociferously now that he has been wounded. And never forget that from the mouth of Trump will usher forth more lies, more evil, and more danger for democracy.

As Jesus warns, "It is what comes out of the mouth that defiles."[11]

10. Prov 21:23.
11. Matt 15:11.

Imagine This Great Cloud of Baptist Witnesses Around the Resolute Desk

WO IMAGES CROWD INTO my mind. One is of President Donald Trump sitting at the *Resolute* desk in the Oval Office, surrounded by a group of evangelical leaders. The other image is the cover artwork of Margaret M. Mitchell's *The Heavenly Trumpet*. The painting, by Leonidas Ananiades, depicts Saint John of Chrysostom at his desk writing a sermon. Standing behind him, peering over his shoulder is Saint Paul, his muse.

In Greek mythology, the "Muses" were the nine daughters of Zeus and Mnemosyne, who presided over the arts and sciences. As Trump attacks the arts and science, the unmistakable influence and inspiration of MAGA Evangelicals takes solid shape.

The gathering of all the president's muses represents a virulent idolatry opposed to the message of the gospel of Jesus Christ. He could not have picked worse muses: Christian nationalism, a fake American history inspired by David Barton and Robert Jeffress, Seven Mountain Dominionists grasping for political control of all aspects of American life, the "real science" of Ken Ham's creationist movement. These combine with raw political power.

Not since President Dwight Eisenhower combined faith and politics in the 1950s have we witnessed such superficiality in the White House.

Eisenhower had no particular passion for Christianity. Influenced by Billy Graham, Ike finally agreed to join the Presbyterian Church. Historian Kevin Kruse relates the incident in *One Nation Under God*.

Eisenhower had agreed to be baptized at National Presbyterian only after the pastor, Edward L. R. Elson, promised to be discreet.

But as Eisenhower wrote angrily in his diary, "We were scarcely home before the fact was being publicized, by the pastor, to the hilt."

The president screamed to his press secretary, Jim Hagerty, "You go and tell that goddam minister that if he gives out one more story about my religious faith I won't join his goddam church!"[1]

Yet Eisenhower, guided by Evangelicals and corporate executives, molded the facade of a Christian America.

Trump's Court Preachers

The Christianity represented by Trump's muses is, at best, as fake and superficial as the gold gilding Trump has splattered all over the place. At worst, it is as pagan as Greek mythology. At least Eisenhower confined his religious outbursts to adding "In God We Trust" to our money—an inadvertent nod to America's real god—and "One nation under God" to our pledge. Eisenhower's Christian movement, like Trump's, was fueled by Evangelicals and corporate executives.

For instance, televangelist Paula White noticed two gold cherub figurines Trump had added to the Oval Office. White, a fan of angels, later offered people a chance to receive seven Easter angels for a one-thousand-dollar contribution to her ministry.

White told Fox and Friends during Holy Week her White House Faith Office has hosted more than one thousand faith leaders in less than one hundred days. One of those was related to Easter, just days before Trump sent out his own Easter blessing: "Happy Easter to all, including the Radical Left Lunatics who are fighting and scheming so hard to bring Murderers, Drug Lords, Dangerous Prisoners, the Mentally Insane, and well known MS-13 Gang Members and Wife Beaters, back into our Country."[2] And so forth.

Yet Pastor Robert Jeffress of First Baptist Dallas—called "Trump's apostle" by *Texas Monthly*—has defended every Trump mistake, transgression, act of cruelty, and lie. He recently claimed Trump is "doing more to celebrate the true meaning of Easter than any president in history."[3]

1. Kruse, *One Nation Under God*, 73.
2. Hassel, "Deranged Donald Trump."
3. Robert Jeffress, "@POTUS is doing more."

Imagine Easter as God's revenge instead of the resurrection defeating death and hell.

MAGA Evangelicals stand in line to stand next to this president in the Oval Office. There's Jackson Laymeyer, an Oklahoma pastor who has said the Constitution is built on the Bible.[4]

There's Jentezen Franklin, an evangelist and senior pastor of the multisite megachurch Free Chapel in Georgia, who told Trump, "We believe you're a vessel," and "You're a chosen vessel," comparing Trump to the apostle Paul. "You're a chosen vessel."[5]

Other prominent Trump pastors include Jack Graham, pastor of Prestonwood Baptist Church in Plano, Texas, and former Southern Baptist Convention president; Samuel Rodriguez and Tony Suarez of the National Hispanic Christian Leadership Conference; and televangelist Mark Burns. Also in Trump's circle of Christians are conservative activists like singer Sean Feucht; Gary Bauer, president of the conservative advocacy organization American Values; and David Barton, evangelical author and WallBuilders founder.

A Gathering of Baptists

In my alternative historical imagination, I see a group of Baptists gathered from the communion of saints around President Trump at the Resolute Desk.

I asked historian Bill Leonard what Baptists he would place around the Resolute Desk. Here's his list:

Roger Williams deserves top billing. As Leonard observes, "I know he didn't stay a Baptist, but his voice for religious liberty as a Baptist makes him a major contributor to what once was Baptist identity for religious freedom."[6]

Williams suggested Native Americans were the sole owners of the American land and should be compensated for it. Imagine Trump's response to Williams as opposed to the voices of his anti-immigrant, nativist-supporting MAGA Evangelicals.

---

4. Dias, "Far-Right Christian Quest."

5. Franklin, "Always an honor"; Montgomery, "Trump Tells Christian Nationalist Leaders."

6. Bill Leonard, email message to author, Apr. 21, 2025.

After his expulsion from the colony, Williams survived a bitter winter with the aid of the Narragansetts. True to his convictions, Williams purchased land from them. He founded Providence, Rhode Island, of which he said, "I desired it might be a shelter for persons distressed of conscience. . . . I communicated my said purchase unto my loving friends, . . . who then desired to take shelter here with me."[7]

Williams also insisted that non-Christians could be good citizens. He argued that "Jews, Turks or anti-Christians" can be "loving and helpful neighbors, fair and just dealers, true and loyal to the civil governments."[8]

John Clarke helped Williams establish the Baptist church in Rhode Island. In his *Ill News from New-England*, Clarke wrote, "No such believer . . . hath any liberty, much less Authority, from his Lord, to smite his fellow servant, nor yet with outward force, or arms of flesh, to constrain, or restrain his Conscience."[9]

Next, let's bring John Leland to the Oval Office. His influence on the writers of the Constitution, especially the First Amendment, puts him next to Williams with his hand on Trump's right shoulder. Leonard reminds us, "Leland lobbied—no, hounded—the founding fathers for what he called the First Amendment." Students of government and democracy say we are experiencing a Constitutional crisis. Leland proclaimed, "Bible Christians and Deists have an equal plea against self-named Christians, who . . . tyrannize over the consciences of others, under the specious garb of religion and good order."[10]

Next, let's bring in William Carey, whose Baptist globalism represents the Baptist passion for global missionary work. He would have a lot to say to Trump, who once referred to certain African nations as "shithole countries."

Then Adoniram Judson and Ann Hasseltine Judson with their world vision. I'm confident the Judsons would thrill at the influx of Burmese immigrants who have come to the United States. Most of the Burmese immigrants are Baptists. Since 2000, more than 188,095 have been admitted to the US.[11] The mission field has come home to do mission work

---

7. Leonard, *Baptist Ways*, 74.

8. Williams, *Bloudy Tenent of Persecution*, 109.

9. Armstrong and Armstrong, *Baptists in America*, 71.

10. Leonard, *Baptist Ways*, 130; Leland, *Writings*, 294.

11. Burmese American Community Institute, "Burmese Population."

in America. They represent the positive potential of immigrants in opposition to the violent immigration policies of Trumpism.

Next, we should summon Fannie Lou Hamer and Martin Luther King Jr. to speak for civil rights. Hamer famously told white Americans, "I am sick and tired of being sick and tired."[12] MLK had the dream for a diverse and integrated America. Trump is trying to turn King's dream into a nightmare.

And who better to speak to Trump's macho male idiocy and his relentless attacks on education than Nannie Helen Burroughs—African American Baptist educator. Burroughs founded the National Title and Profession School for Women and Girls in Washington, DC, in 1909. She was a trailblazer in promoting the leadership of women in churches.

Then let's add Harry Emerson Fosdick, who understood the illiberal spirit of fundamentalists, a spirit now resplendent among MAGA Evangelicals. In his famous sermon, "Shall the Fundamentalists Win?" he said of the fundamentalists, "Their apparent intention is to drive out of the evangelical churches men and women of liberal opinions."[13]

And finally, let's invite Will Campbell because every Baptist group requires one curmudgeon. Campbell thunders, "Shame on those fat-cat false prophets spewing their toxic rhetoric, trying to control every facet of American life with a selective reading of the Bible. That's blasphemy. It's idolatry."[14]

Just imagine if this great cloud of witnesses were guiding the president rather than the MAGA minions Trump surrounds himself with.

This imagined gathering of Baptists may not persuade a change in a president famous for believing he never has done anything requiring him to repent, but I think even Donald Trump would be awed in the presence of such saints of Almighty God.

12. Say It Plain, "Fannie Lou Hamer."
13. Fosdick, "Shall the Fundamentalists Win?"
14. Campbell, *Soul Among Lions*, 20.

Here Are All the Words Trump
Wants Banned—In One Article

AMERICAN DEMOCRACY FACES ITS greatest peril since 1861. President Donald Trump and his Project 2025–infused zealots are ripping through two centuries of progress in human rights, civil rights, sexual rights, and democratic rights. Historically, race always has been the elephant in our culture.

Trump's inquisitors, leaving nothing to chance, are banning words. I have poured the list of Trump's banned words into a gallon bucket. I have shaken the bucket as if it were filled with all the possible winning tickets of a lottery and jump-started a sentence that led to a paragraph, and a paragraph that led to this article. I have used every word on the banned list except *obesity*. Oops, I used it as well. And more words have been added to this list since I started writing.

Some of these word-scrubbing zealots are more zealous than their superiors. They make mistakes so egregious they have to put back some words, pictures, and stories due to public outrage. When Secretary of Defense Pete Hegseth banned the books of Maya Angelou but kept Hitler's *Mein Kampf* on the shelves of the library of the Naval Academy, more than eyebrows raised.

I concluded the banned words are a direct attack on democracy. Instead, they are excellent words providing a foundation for celebrating democracy and human rights. These words should not be banned but debated, discussed, wrestled with, deliberated, and hammered out. I gladly accept my identity as a promoter of democracy and confess a sense of trauma even reading a list of banned words.

Walt Whitman's contagious democratic spirit fills his poetry: "O Democracy, . . . for you, for you I am trilling these songs."[1] I consider it poetic justice that we can be led to renew our democratic freedoms by a queer socialist poet capable of saving America from itself.

The list of banned words concentrates on four areas that are an attack on America's true democratic values.

Support Anti-Racism

Democracy has no space in its diverse and beautiful house for racism. A person can swear on a stack of King James Bibles she is not racist, but when she has a meltdown over words like all-inclusive, anti-racist, biases, diversity, equity, indigenous people, and inequality, the racial bias shines a light on the deeply embedded racist.

No matter how many times a person says, "Everyone who knows me knows I'm not a racist, but I just don't like to hear people talk about injustice, inequities, minorities, multiculturalism, and oppression," there's an implied confession.

The new face of racism in America doesn't hide under white robes or burn crosses. Now, it hides behind denial and banning words. But scratch beneath the surface, and there's old Jim Crow with his loaded biases including implicit biases. There's a sense MAGA misses segregation.

Since the passage of the Civil Rights Act, Americans have, first reluctantly and then robustly, promoted the rights of African Americans. Affirmative action signaled a willingness to start making up for the huge disadvantages African American students faced in education. Attention was given to minority enrollment and minority hiring opportunities. Progressives long have been supporters of minority opportunity and have gladly supported minority-serving institutions.

America was proud to fly the flag of inclusion, to embrace inclusive leadership, increase diversity, and overcome inequalities. You can count on progressives fostering inclusivity. When Barack Obama was elected president in 2008, some thought America had accomplished Martin's dream. As important as it was to elect a Black man, not once but twice, as our president, it didn't mean the tide of racism had permanently turned.

Only in 2016 did we learn that one man, Donald Trump, whose only ideology is white supremacy, would take advantage of the latent racism

---

1. "For You O Democracy," in Whitman, *Leaves of Grass*, 99.

in our nation to win the presidency, not once but twice. Under Trump, every gain we thought we had made permanent in civil rights was in danger of being demolished. White supremacy now works to exploit tribal loyalties.

At least ten words are on the list directly using variations of race: *race* and *ethnicity, racial, racial diversity, racial identity, racial inequality, racial justice, racially,* and *racism.* The incongruity reminds me of a mother in a Southern short story who believed "if you don't discuss something, it doesn't exist."[2]

This heteronormative, masculine movement attempts to hide its ideology of male supremacy by banning male domination. It is like a group of Southern Baptist pastors pretending the SBC is not male dominated. Among the banned words that cry MAGA denial, sensitivity to reality, and easily jarred feelings, I discovered the following words: *underappreciated, underprivileged, underrepresented, undeserved, underserved, understudied, under studied, undervalued, victim, victims,* and *vulnerable populations.*

The anti-DEI fervor of Trump and his surrogates has moved with remarkable and cruel speed. High-ranking African American women have been fired from their positions. President Trump has fired Carla Hayden, first woman and first Black person to lead the Library of Congress.

The word-banning fever reaches epidemic proportion when liberals promote diversity, equity, and inclusion. The banned list becomes repetitive: *diverse, diverse backgrounds, diverse communities, diverse community, diverse group, diverse groups, diversified, diversify, equity, equality, equitable, equitableness, entitlement, inclusion, inclusive, inclusive leadership, inclusiveness,* and *inclusivity.*

One interesting word or acronym on the list is *BIPOC.* The meaning: Black, Indigenous, People of Color. Throw in *Black* and *Black and Latinx* and you have a full-grown racism. Two odd synonyms on the list are *key groups* and *key people.* And what is the MAGA addiction to acronyms? *DEI, DEIA, DEIAB, DEIJ, MSI, EEJ, EJ, GBV, LGBT, LGBTQ, Mx, MSI,* and *msm.* One gets the sense MAGA is stitched together by lies, conspiracy theories, revenge, slogans, and acronyms.

They aim for a homogenized all-white culture void of distressing mentions of indigenous people and indigenous community. Trump and MAGA want nothing to do with special populations.

---

2. "Tongues of Fire," in Smith, *Me and My Baby,* 88.

Trump attempts to disrupt our democratic support for marginalized groups we are not members of by placing *allyship* on the banned list. As white progressives, it is part of our calling to support minorities, immigrants, LGBTQ, women, Native Americans, and every group suffering from oppression and discrimination.

No doubt *sociocultural* and *socioeconomic* show up in the list as manifestations of MAGA fear of multiculturalism, diversity, and differences.

MAGA tips its hand at serous disdain for a diverse culture by adding *cultural competence, cultural differences, cultural heritage, cultural relevance, cultural sensitivity, culturally appropriate,* and *culturally responsive* to the banned words list.

A residual hate bubbles under the MAGA surface. This is why they fight so hard to preserve the freedom of hate speech.

Support LGBTQ

MAGA has more white rage against LGBTQ people than any other group. The banned list insists on a subtle mockery with the phrase *men who have sex with men* (an allusion to Lev 18:22 and an utter disregard of Acts 10:15—"What God has made clean, you must not call profane").

They struggle in all areas of human sexuality from abortion to transgender identity. MAGA has created an imaginary but frightening "gender war." The usual MAGA fear of feminism also includes *sex, sexual preferences, sexuality, nonbinary,* and *they/them*. Evangelical repression of sex is now coming up through the sewers of clergy *sexual misconduct, sexual misbehavior,* and *sexual misunderstanding*.

For decades MAGA fought to define a human embryo as a child. Now, they fight over gender assigned at birth—male or female. Somehow MAGA has nightmares about the occurrence of intersex—having sex organs or other sexual characteristics that are not clearly male or female, that are a combination of typical male and female organs, or that do not correspond to the individual's chromosomal sex.

Understandably, a group willing to go to war over public restrooms, having previously fought over the closet, would not embrace the term *chestfeed*, a gender-neutral term.

While MAGA Evangelicals have a decided and century-old disdain for biology, when it comes to sexuality they are suddenly determined opponents of the words *biologically female* and *biologically male*.

Support Science

Trump is the most powerful man in the world, and he is a climate-denier. The banned words swirling around the issue of global warming demonstrate that this is about more than words because Trump is acting irresponsibly by ignoring and attempting to destroy research and progress in defeating global warming.

Trump mocks the idea of *clean energy, climate crisis,* and *climate science.* His slogan, "Drill, baby, drill" is a direct slap in the face of the attempts of our scientific community to decrease our dependence on fossil fuels before we become fossils, as did the dinosaurs.

Climate deniers are a determined bunch of politicians, engaging in an all-out effort to place barriers to any attempt to ward off the coming climate apocalypse.

Anti-science now controls the Department of Health and Human Services under Robert F. Kennedy Jr. That a nonscience, nonphysician conspiracy theorist is the director of HHS boggles the mind. Kennedy recently went swimming in a creek with high bacteria levels, including E. coli. He has a strange aversion to fluoride in water. He continues to ignore the measles epidemic even as it spreads. He promotes conspiracy theories about the cause of autism, pontificates on mental health, and promotes unscientific ideas on dietary guidelines / ultra-processed foods, peanut allergies, and vaccines.

Of course, *people-centered care, person-centered,* and *person-centered care* make the list. People-centered care extends the concept of patient-centered care to individuals, families, communities, and society.

The disregard of the Trump administration for the well-being of all Americans shows up in the banning of *health disparity* and *health equity.* The terms refer to everyone having a fair and just opportunity to attain the highest possible level of good health.

The banned words tell us how little the Trump administration cares about *environmental justice* and *environmental quality.* The most crucial of all the dangers bearing down on our planet is not a giant meteor falling from the sky but our own negligence in caring for the environment.

The administration's lack of concern for health shows up in the banning of *Cancer Moonshot, COVID-19, science-based, stem cell* or *fetal tissue research, health disparity,* and *health equity.* For example, Cancer Moonshot was a 2016 initiative aimed at more scientific discovery in cancer research with the goal of preventing more than four million cancer deaths by 2047. In 2022, 608,366 people died of cancer. Anyone not wanting to do everything scientifically possible to eradicate cancer deaths seems anti-humane. But a determined MAGA has banned NCI (National Cancer Institute) budget as a topic of deliberation.

Support Democracy

We must find ways to advance democratic ends. One way of doing this job is to reject the banned words and use them in our speeches, essays, books, articles, and sermons. I see the banned words as tropes that make a democratic turn toward preserving human rights and civil rights.

The banned words include anti-democracy words: *activism, activists, advocacy, advocate,* and *advocates.* Trump's attack on law firms he deems his enemy illustrates his disdain for advocacy. So does his relentless attack on judges and the Constitution.

I have questions about the list: Why is *pregnant people* on the banned list? Why put *commercial sex worker* and *prostitute* on the list? Does MAGA really believe they can eradicate the world's oldest profession? Placing *marijuana* on the list merely confuses me.

Why ban words such as *disabilities, disability,* and *disabled*? (Maybe this has to do with Trump's aversion to disabled people. He mocked a *New York Times* reporter with a disability.) This helps explain why *accessible* and *accessibility* are banned words.

Are you serious? The *Gulf of Mexico* is on the banned list. I suppose Trump wasn't satisfied with denying the Associated Press to participate in press conferences.

Why the angst over the word *systemic*? My best guess is MAGA is sensitive about the reality of systemic racism as it exposes how they may not be individually racist but are racist to the core in cultural, ethnic, and political ways.

Why does discussion of federal policy make the list? No authoritarian administration desires discussion or deliberation, only fealty.

Why would any sane person oppose the word *belong* or *sense of belonging*?

Some Final Words

People who despise diversity only know how to celebrate sameness, a mind-numbing monotonous sameness void of the richness of African Americans (Blacks), Hispanics, Asians, gays, lesbians, bisexuals, transgender people, and queers. Ours is a rich and multicultural nation blessed by the God who made of one blood all nations of the earth.

The land of purple-colored mountains holds within her bosom the richness of indigenous communities. Native American reservations now dotted with casinos show in living color the American struggle to care adequately for others.

The church, having inherited the universal gospel of Jesus, is called to be the clear, authentic voice of inclusion. The early church struggled with inclusion before the gentiles were admitted as full members.

In my self-assessment, I heed the advice of historian David Blight and

> pick up Whitman's *Song of Myself*, all 51 pages, from the opening line, "celebrate myself, and sing myself," to his musings on the luck of merely being alive. Keep going to a few pages later when a "runaway slave" enters Whitman's home and the poet gazes into his "revolving eyes," and nurses "the galls of his neck and ankles," and then to his embrace of "primeval" complete democracy midway in the song, where he accepts "nothing which all cannot have." Finally read to the ending, where the poet finds blissful oblivion, bequeathing himself "to the dirt to grow from the grass I love." Whitman's "sign of democracy" is everywhere and in everything. The democratic and the authoritarian instinct are both deep within us, forever at war.[3]

I affirm I have not been under the influence of alcohol or opioids. I have pointed out the disparity in Trump and MAGA's relentless campaign against democracy. If my defense of democracy puts me at risk, so be it. Others may stereotype me as a typical progressive, but I am at peace with my expression.

There is nothing to fear in the words on the banned list, and I have taken it on myself to move them all to the celebrated words list. I believe all words should be free to walk in the corridors of all minds at all times. There are more than a million words in the English language, and I don't want to lose even one.

3. Blight, "'Lost Cause' Myth."

Epilogue: A Pair of Conversations

T HIS IS AN EPILOGUE, which means—following the Latin *epilogus* and the Greek *epilogos*—"a conclusion." The primary meaning suggests saying something "in addition." I could not think of a better way of saying "in addition" than offering an email conversation between William Vance Trollinger and myself. Trollinger is a history professor at the University of Dayton. In addition to teaching courses (including PhD seminars), he directs the Core Integrated Studies Program.

Talking about Donald Trump and his evangelical army has been of more value to me than any other genre. Trollinger has been my main conversational partner for more than fifteen years. Trollinger has the gift of pulling from me the essence of what I have been trying to say about Trump for more than a decade.

Beyond pointing out the obvious vices of lying, defrauding, attacking, lacking any sense of decorum, and having little attachment to the truth, my main contention has been to evaluate Trump's actions and rhetoric as the "embodiment of evil." For me, Trump fits the analogy of the "Evil Lover" in Plato's *Phaedrus*, the transactional, "might-is-right" pragmatism of Plato's Callicles, the "evil woman" so prominent in the Old Testament book of Proverbs, and the pictures of the evil one found throughout the Psalms.

Trollinger published our conversations on his *Righting America* blog.[1] He probed my understanding of Trump as a creature of evangelical faith from my first Trump book, *The Immaculate Mistake: How Evangelicals Gave Birth to Donald Trump*, and my second Trump book, *Good and Evil in the Garden of Democracy*.

---

1. www.rightingamerica.net.

TROLLINGER: In my preface to your book—a preface I was honored to write—I noted that "the Rev. Dr. Rodney Kennedy is the quintessential example of a Protestant preacher who cannot be shoehorned into either the conservative or the liberal 'party.' Instead, Kennedy is (to quote from his introduction) the ex-fundamentalist 'misfit who believes Jesus, who he was and is, what he taught and preached.'"[2] Could you elaborate on this point, in the process explaining how you became the Jesus-believing ex-fundamentalist misfit?

KENNEDY: My original impulse was my dissatisfaction with "biblical inerrancy," which seemed to be more about the Bible than Jesus. The longer I actually read and dealt with biblical texts, the more I realized that our faith has no foundation other than Jesus. This put me in a distinct minority in my Southern Baptist tribe. Louisiana Baptist College, of all places, provided me with the intellectual framework to escape the strictures of my fundamentalism. My religious studies professors opened my mind to new possibilities. As laughable as it may sound, I changed sides forever when I realized that Cain found a wife, given that I had always been taught there was Adam and Eve and two sons and no other humans. This started me on a pilgrimage that led me to the far left bank of liberalism. After a few less than helpful years, I didn't exactly move back to the middle. Instead, I reclaimed some of the icons of my youthful Christian experience. By that I mean that I reclaimed the Bible as the primary text for my faith, but not the Bible as read by fundamentalists. I was disenchanted by a liberal faith that basically dismissed the Bible as too patriarchal, classist, xenophobic, and bloodthirsty. Accepting that the Bible reflected all those cultural factors, I still knew the Bible was the book for me. The critical study of the Bible gave me the tools I needed to investigate this history of abuse and take the Bible seriously. This made me a "misfit" among liberals, and thus I was now suspect in both tribes. I applied Flannery O'Connor's term "misfit" to my ministry without pressing her analogy too far. Later I also, after reading Cornel West, saw myself as an "outcast." An outcast is someone not considered to be part of the normal world. I embrace this stance in my preaching and in my writing.

TROLLINGER: One of the fascinating things about your book is that you argue that "evangelicals have been misunderstood, mischaracterized, and maligned as a bunch of dummies, a multitude of misguided

---

2. William Trollinger, cited in Kennedy, *Immaculate Mistake*, xi.

Christians easily conned."[3] Why do you make this point, and why does it matter?

KENNEDY: I make this point because all Christians are "evangelicals" in the biblical sense and the historical sense, but not in the contemporary political sense. The media didn't seem to have the theological/historical perception necessary to explain evangelicals, and this bothered me a great deal. In 2016 nothing came as a greater shock than the wholesale commitment by evangelicals to Donald Trump. At the same time, I found myself, as an evangelical (ABC USA) disgruntled by the media coverage of evangelicals. The template of evangelicals, forged in the steel-trap mind of H. L. Mencken, remains the go-to description now. H. L. Mencken had written, his tongue dipped in vitriol, that the South (a synonym for evangelical) consisted of a "cesspool of Baptists, a miasma of Methodists, snake charmers, phony real estate operators, and syphilitic evangelists."[4] A liberal media piled on the stereotypes and added that evangelicals were mostly poor, uneducated, angry white working-class folk.

As a Southerner and an evangelical, I found myself insulted as the indictment of my kinfolk unfolded in the media. The condescension was almost unbearable. The sneering, mocking, insulting barbs were made more painful by the undisguised glee that pundits displayed in attacking evangelicals. The result bordered on a sense of ressentiment—a group of likeminded persons (the media) enjoying one another enjoying being cruel to evangelicals. "We so obviously despise them, we so obviously condescend to them," the conservative social scientist Charles Murray, who co-wrote *The Bell Curve*, told *The New Yorker*. "The only slur you can use at a dinner party and get away with is to call somebody a redneck—that won't give you any problems in Manhattan." Celebrity chef Anthony Bourdain minced no words in his gumbo of contempt: "red-state, gun-country, working-class Americans as ridiculous and morons and rubes."[5]

Somewhere in the back of my mind Garth Brooks was wailing, "I got friends in low places." I confess being injured by these attacks. In this moment of pathos, I decided to challenge the conclusions of the liberal media. *The Immaculate Mistake*'s originating idea was born in the heat of this hot-blooded moment. Not to mistake me as an evangelical defender, I attempt to make the case that evangelicals have been in the business of

---

3. Kennedy, *Immaculate Mistake*, 3.

4. H. L. Mencken, cited in Ketchin, *Christ-Haunted Landscape*, xi.

5. Packer, "Hilary Clinton."

bringing to life, of giving birth, to Donald Trump for more than a century of resentment, mistrust, and anger. My defense of the stereotypes gives way to my own assessment of what I believe is the evangelical sellout.

TROLLINGER: What do you mean by the title of your book, and on what basis do you claim that "evangelicals are the organ grinders" and "Trump is the monkey"?[6]

KENNEDY: I believe that the appearance of Donald Trump was the culmination of almost a century of fundamentalist/evangelical attempts to be in charge, to force the rest of the nation into their template of faith. In my view, the moment the evangelicals walked out of the courthouse in Dayton, Tennessee, they returned to the woods and hammered out an alternate universe. They nurtured a deep resentment that I traced from the Scopes Trial to the election of Donald Trump. My thought was that evangelicals were the grandparents and parents of Donald Trump. I investigated numerous evangelical leaders and finally selected three representatives of this version of faith: Billy Sunday, J. Frank Norris, and Jerry Falwell. In my mind, the conservative evangelicals had been looking for a "strong man" to enable them to exact revenge for the loss they perceived happened to them in evolution. In fact, I believe that every anti-science stance the evangelicals take, including the refusal to wear a Covid mask, is rooted in the originating anti-evolution stance. Ken Ham and Robert Jeffress frequently assail evolution as the root cause of every evil that has come down the pike in our culture. Evangelical dissatisfaction with President Jimmy Carter (they sold him out for Ronald Reagan), with Bush I and Bush II, with the conservative appointees to the Supreme Court who refused to do evangelical bidding, led them to seek a candidate who was, in the words of Robert Jeffress, "the meanest s. o. g." in the country. What comes out here is the evangelical lust for winning at any costs and with any ally. They betray their own faith by using the weapons of the devil for what they deem good ends. In other words, faced with the temptation like those faced by Jesus in the wilderness, they accepted the devil's deal. The devil didn't just come down to Georgia; the devil came to the entire South and the entire evangelical nation formed by southern religion and offered them control and they said "Yes, yes, yes!"

My title is thus a bit of satire or sarcasm aimed at the self-righteousness of evangelicals who believe they possess a holiness that all other religious groups lack. The word "immaculate" seemed a perfect fit for

6. Kennedy, *Immaculate Mistake*, 10.

a bunch of "inerrantists." The idea that Trump was their baby led me to the trope that evangelicals were the organ grinder and Trump was their monkey. The liberal media was wrong, in my view, to think that the evangelicals were duped, deceived, and made fools of by Trump. Instead, the two were a perfect match of perfidy—each using the other for dubious means. Trump and the evangelicals engage in what rhetorical scholars dubbed "ressentiment"[7] and "jouissance."[8] Trump and the evangelicals nurture and cultivate resentment and deep anger. Trump took out this resentment on the media, the liberals, and all other groups despised by evangelicals. At a Trump rally, you can witness the speaker and his audience enjoying Trump's cruelty and doing it together—"jouissance."

TROLLINGER: Given your knowledge and love of the Bible, I know it infuriates you that evangelicals have mangled the Bible in their defense of Trump. Could you give a couple of examples?

KENNEDY: When Pentecostal journalist/preacher/evangelist Lance Wallnau suggested that Trump was the new Cyrus, I knew that the attempt to make Trump "God's anointed" would be a full-blown campaign. Wallnau said that when he realized that Trump would be the 45th president of the United States, he was led by the Holy Spirit to read Isaiah 45.[9] I have no idea why he didn't read Psalm 45, Jeremiah 45, or Ezekiel 45. He read Isaiah 45 because it fit his notion that Trump, like Cyrus, was God's anointed. No one seemed to notice that Trump was nothing like Cyrus. All that mattered was the sound bite: "Trump Is God's Anointed." From here, the full-orbed defense of Trump bellowed forth from the pulpit of First Baptist Church Dallas and the Rev. Dr. Robert Jeffress. Every mistake, every slip, every awful word, and every dreadful deed of Trump was defended and glossed over by Jeffress. In defending Trump's payoff to a porn star, Jeffress even invented an 11th commandment, "Thou shalt not have sex with a porn star," and said that even if Trump had violated that commandment, what evangelicals supported were his wonderful policies. At the same time, evangelical preachers unleashed a veritable army of biblical tropes for Trump. Trump was lauded as King David. This shows a shallow reading of the story of David because David repented of his sexual abuse of "the wife of Uriah," while Trump swore he didn't need to repent. Trump was heralded as Samson and again the reading

---

7. Kelly, "Rhetoric of Ressentiment," 2.

8. Andrejevic, "Jouissance of Trump," 651.

9. Fea, *Believe Me*, 112–13.

is shallow. Samson was deceived by a beautiful woman and then pulled down the temple of the Philistines on all of his enemies. This may, in light of January 6, be exactly the Trump trope that we should utilize.

TROLLINGER: In your conclusion you suggest possible rhetorics that could be used against white evangelicals and their "secular preacher," Donald Trump. Could you say a little about this?

KENNEDY: An important rhetorical strategy is "naming" the negative and destructive tropes of Trump. As a debater I am aware that an argument stands in the course of a debate until it is refuted. The false assertions and outright lies of Trump need to be refuted over and over again. A second strategy is to align Trump supporters with his racist, xenophobic rhetoric. Trump supporters are endorsing and celebrating a legacy of white supremacy, homophobia, and misogyny that we thought had passed from the scene. In the face of evangelical denials of these behaviors, the pedagogy of shame from civic virtue and progressive thought has to continue with full-orbed zeal. We must recognize the danger that Trump branding, braggadocio, and demolition rhetoric creates for democracy. This means that the most positive strategy is the rhetoric of real democracy. When Trump scapegoats, we name and shame. We offer fierce resistance to his hateful, hurtful rhetoric. By showing our nation the vitality and energy of real democracy, by engaging in empathy and compassion, we not only contrast with Trump's rhetoric of hatred, we offer a viable alternative. Frank and honest speech is an important part of our democracy. By realizing this, perhaps more rhetors will be willing to engage in American democracy as truth tellers.

TROLLINGER: Could you talk about your current take on Trump?

KENNEDY: When I finished *The Immaculate Mistake*, I realized that I had not gone far enough in my critique of evangelicals. What was even more pressing was a move beyond insisting—as rhetorical scholars had done—that Trump was a perverted populist, a demagogue, a serial liar, and a danger to democracy. In *Good and Evil in the Garden of Democracy*, I develop the argument that Trump is the personification of evil: theologically, philosophically, politically, and rhetorically. He is the essence of what Sheldon Wolin labels "inverted totalitarianism."

Trump is the Evil One incarnate.[10]

---

10. Interview quoted from Trollinger, "*Immaculate Mistake*."

TROLLINGER: Having just written and published *The Immaculate Mistake: How Evangelicals Gave Birth to Donald Trump*, what prompted you to write *Good and Evil in the Garden of Democracy*?

KENNEDY: Stanley Hauerwas, in the preface to *Working with Words*, says, "The world probably does not need another book by me."[11] Those words made me ponder whether the world needs another book about Donald Trump. My answer, as this work makes it obvious, was yes. My reasons for writing about Trump are many. Trump is still a danger, a menace to democracy. I am convinced that Trump remains an important subject for evaluation because he has created a certain spirit in our political environment, and I believe it is toxic. Most of all, I write because I am a dissident, a dissident in the description offered by Vaclav Havel: "You do not become 'dissident' just because you decide one day to take up this most unusual career. You are thrown into it by your personal sense of responsibility, combined with a complex set of external circumstances. You are cast out of the existing structures and placed in a position of conflict with them. It begins as an attempt to do your work well and ends with being branded an enemy of society."[12]

TROLLINGER: Befitting your PhD in rhetoric and your lifetime as a Baptist minister, in this book you make great use of current rhetorical scholarship as well as Plato, Proverbs, and the Psalms. Could you say a little about your research methodology?

KENNEDY: I write more as a preacher than as a scholar because I have been writing sermons for sixty years. I find it impossible to write without incorporating biblical texts. When I read biblical narratives, I read them metaphorically. I am not locked into a reduced literalism. This enlivens my biblical imagination, a technique that I learned first from African American preachers like Gardner Taylor.

For example, the story of Paul preaching to the philosophers in Athens amazes me. On the one hand, there is the astounding boldness of St. Paul to take on the embedded wisdom of a long-standing pagan philosophical tradition. Then there is the analogical reality that we now find ourselves in the same place. We too are attempting to speak to a generation of "philosophers" who mock and deride the Christian faith. I find it fascinating to consider the epistemological possibilities that are presented to Christians preaching in a secular age. Here I combine the

11. Hauerwas, *Working with Words*, ix.

12. Havel, *Power of the Powerless*, 58.

study of Charles Taylor, especially his *A Secular Age*, and the work of philosopher James K. A. Smith, *How (Not) to Be Secular*. They raise the question of how we are to witness in a secular age, an age that considers all talk about God as "babbling." In fact, I just preached a sermon on this very idea:

> The word seems a perfect fit for the old story of the tower of Babel. It's a story explaining how people came to speak so many languages, but as a metaphor it rings true. We are babblers and the towers we have constructed; towers of grandness, wealth, and power are falling. We have not been the same since 9/11 when the Twin Towers—symbol of our financial wealth, were destroyed by war criminals. Now, we are scared that the economy will tank, and another Great Depression is around the corner. And, out of fear, we babble. That's what some scared people do—they talk incessantly and with a serious dose of paranoia.
>
> Charles Taylor claims that our world is a world suspended between the enchantment of transcendence—a default setting of believing in God—and "the malaise of immanence," a flat space where there is no God.[13] If we don't pay attention to the swelling numbers of the exclusive humanists, there is not going to be a church. Immanence is destroying transcendence. If some people in the house of God don't sacrifice some time, some intellectual sweat, some thoughtful effort to communicate with this Age, this house is going to be destroyed. Some people are going to have to step up and say, "There is still God in this house." And the God in this house loves gays, transgenders, women, minorities, immigrants, and the whole world of human flesh. It's that simple. That puts the ball in our court. In the minds, mouths, and lives of believers—which is exactly where it belongs.

TROLLINGER: I found this statement particularly striking: "To describe Trump as a demagogue, a psycho, or a fascist retreats to a rhetorical safe zone. To assert as I do that Donald Trump is evil, the incarnation of evil, is to say something about the ethos of an actual human being."[14] What do you mean by "rhetorical safe zone," why have scholars and other observers stayed in that safe zone, and what has caused you to leave the safe zone?

KENNEDY: There has always been a sort of unwritten rule in rhetorical studies not to use the criticism of a person's ethos as a critique of the "person." In psychology this is called the "Goldwater Rule": it is

---

13. Smith, *How (Not) to Be Secular*, loc. 88.

14. Kennedy, *Good and Evil*, 118.

unprofessional and unethical to psychoanalyze public figures whom you have not analyzed personally. Rhetorical scholars have exercised a similar caution. In my research I discovered that rhetorical scholars were of one mind in asserting the dangers of Donald Trump. They have found him to be a demagogue, a charlatan, a bully, a deranged populist, a rhetorical pervert, a demolition machine. But then I realized that the rhetorical scholars had not gone as far as necessary. It dawned on me that Trump was the definition of embodied evil. He was too dangerous not to expose. Safety was ignored, and I started writing *Good and Evil* out of a sense of necessity. The book became an example of the biblical concept of parrhesia—the fearless speaking of the truth to the powers, in the process taking personal and professional risks in order to do one's duty.

TROLLINGER: Speaking of escaping the rhetorical safe zone, you devote a chapter to comparing Donald Trump with Adolf Hitler. And while you repeatedly note that you are not claiming Trump equals Hitler, this is indeed a daring comparison. Why go there, and what do we learn from such a comparison?

KENNEDY: I struggled with my conclusions surrounding Trump, but I was convinced that Kenneth Burke, in his brilliant "The Rhetoric of Hitler's 'Battle,'" offered a challenge I could not avoid. The words startled me: "Let us try to discover what kind of 'medicine' this medicine-man has concocted, that we may know, with greater accuracy, exactly what to guard against, if we are to forestall the concocting of similar medicine in America."[15]

Even more convincing was Burke's argument that Hitler's appeals relied upon "a bastardization of fundamentally religious patterns of thought."[16] My head was spinning from my previous work on the "total identification" of Trump and the evangelicals.

I was completely convinced that my line of thought was necessary when I read these words from Burke: "Our job is to find all the ways of making the Hitlerite distortions of religion apparent, in order that politicians of his kind in America be unable to perform a similar swindle."[17]

For me the die was cast. Trump had to face the judgment that he is a "medicine man" selling a "fake salvation."

There was, in retrospect, some deliberate rhetorical satire involved on my part. Trump's favorite rhetorical trope is paralipsis: "I'm not saying,

15. Burke, "Rhetoric of Hitler's Battle," 191.

16. Burke, "Rhetoric of Hitler's Battle," 219.

17. Burke, "Rhetoric of Hitler's Battle," 219.

but I'm just saying."[18] Trump is a master at this rhetorical strategy. Using Trump's brand of paralipsis: I'm not saying Trump is Hitler. I'm just saying that he talks like Hitler, thinks like Hitler, and uses Hitler's rhetorical techniques in ways that make Burke's warning about such a politician gaining power in America became very real.

TROLLINGER: Again and again in the book you make reference to a central question regarding the Trump phenomenon, i.e., how is it that so many Christians, particularly evangelicals, have given themselves over to this evil man? How do you answer this question, and what does this say about the state of Christianity in twenty-first-century America?

KENNEDY: My deepest heartbreak is the selling of the evangelical soul to Trump. I detest evangelical teachings on evolution, creation, the rapture, the end of the world, and the origin of America. I detest their anti-gay, anti-woman, anti-science, anti-history, anti–global warming rants. But I find all of this relatively harmless when compared to accepting the political power offered by Donald Trump.

I am convinced that the evangelicals accepted the gifts of the devil that Jesus rejected in the temptation narrative. Look at Luke's words about the temptation of Jesus. "Then the devil led him up and showed him in an instant all the kingdoms of the world. And the devil said to him, 'To you I will give their glory and all this authority; for it has been given over to me, and I give it to anyone I please. If you, then, will worship me, it will all be yours.'"[19]

Don't you see? The devil tells Jesus that political power has been given to him and he can give it to anyone he pleases. I believe the devil has given that power—that Jesus refused—to evangelicals. In return, they are worshiping him while claiming to worship Jesus. How else can people waving Jesus flags take part in the January 6 invasion of our nation's capital?

In short, evangelicals have not so much given themselves over to Trump as they have surrendered everything to the Evil One. Trump is simply their instrument of gaining power and control over absolutely everything and everyone.

TROLLINGER: You conclude your book with two chapters, "The Rhetorical Good: Vaclav Havel" and "Singing for Democracy" (which focuses a lot on Walt Whitman), that suggest the possibility of a democratic, inclusive,

18. Mercieca, *Demagogue for President*, 10.
19. Luke 4:5–7.

and empathetic rhetoric. Could you elaborate a little on this, and are you hopeful that such a rhetoric could take the place of Trumpian rhetoric?

KENNEDY: Thanks for asking this question. The concluding chapters are the heart of my argument. I have a deep respect for the work of Havel—the dissident poet. He is the political embodiment of St. Paul's "rhetoric of folly."[20] I have written about this previously with my rhetorical colleague Kenneth Zagacki.

My trust in the gospel of Jesus remains rock solid. In my first book, *The Creative Power of Metaphor*, I offered a new rhetoric for preachers—inclusive, empathetic, and democratic. It is the heart of my own theology of preaching. In my research on Walt Whitman, I had the pleasure of reading *In Walt We Trust* by John Marsh. The subtitle of the book puts it exactly right for me: *How a Queer Socialist Poet Can Save America from Itself*. I am adamant that the church has no choice but to dissent vigorously from the anti-gay agenda of evangelicals. My hope is that we will have the boldness to preach the gospel of hospitality, the church as the place that makes a space for God and all the people God created to feel at home.

TROLLINGER: Between books, articles for various outlets (including monthly posts for *rightingamerica*), and sermons—and I am sure I am leaving something out!—you seem to be writing constantly. How do you explain your incredible productivity? Do you ever have a day off?

KENNEDY: I have been practicing the art of writing for more than 60 years. A sermon a week for 60 years equals about 3,000 sermons of 1700 words per sermon. That's 85,000 words per year or the equivalent of a book a year for 60 years. That's more than 5 million words.

I am not aware that I am that productive. I find myself feeling rather "slothful" at times. Writing is so hard, and it requires all my attention. My mind has been trained over all these decades to be prepared for any idea or subject that might cross my mind. There are mornings when I awake and there's an article waiting for me. I sit at the computer and try to type fast enough to keep up with the words tumbling from my mind. I am grateful. By the time I'm 140 I think I will have come close to perfecting these ideals.

I think it is important to produce material from the left wing of the church. I played baseball for about twenty years of my life, and I was a left-handed pitcher. I write left-handed and I write from the progressive

20. Zagacki, "Vaclav Havel," 17.

left-wing of the church. I love the arguments. People think I'm angry, but I'm not. I am delighted to be engaged in ongoing arguments.

As I have reached the age when I am too old to serve as a full-time pastor, I have turned to writing. I write to know what I think. Writing has become my therapist for feeling useless. I want to be involved in the future of the church because church matters and church has a future. And it may not be dominated by the evangelicals. As a sacramentalist, I think the Episcopalians, the Catholics, and the new United Methodist Church (disencumbered by the moralistic conservatives who are rushing to join the Global [?] Methodist Church) will have a lot to say about the shape and vitality of the church.

I write furiously. I think that it may be my unconscious desire to think I can ward off the approach of death, but that discussion would require therapy. When I was young I expressed my desire to die in the pulpit preaching a sermon. I now think no congregation should have to go through that in order for me to satisfy a selfish dream. So I will keep writing and concentrate on how I'm living.[21]

May God deliver us from the demagogic and authoritarian serial liar who now serves as our president.

---

21. Interview quoted from Trollinger, "*Good and Evil.*"

Bibliography

ABC News. "1 in 10 Say It's Acceptable to Hold Neo-Nazi Views." Aug. 21, 2017. https://abcnews.go.com/Politics/28-approve-trumps-response-charlottesville-poll/story?id=49334079.

Achter, Paul. "Great Television: Trump and the Shadow Archetype." In *Faking the News. What Rhetoric Can Teach Us About Donald J. Trump*, edited by Ryan Skinnell. Exeter: Imprint Academic, 2018.

Alexander, Chris, dir. "December 15, 2020." *PBS NewsHour*, Dec. 15, 2020. https://www.pbs.org/video/december-15-2020-pbs-newshour-full-episode-1608008401/.

Allen, Ira J. "Who Owns Donald Trump's Antisemitism?" In *Faking the News. What Rhetoric Can Teach Us About Donald J. Trump*, edited by Ryan Skinnell. Exeter: Imprint Academic, 2018.

Andrejevic, Mark. "The Jouissance of Trump." *Television and New Media* 17 (2016) 651–55.

Applebaum, Anne. "The Oligarchs Who Turn Democracy into Something Else." *Atlantic*, June 9, 2021. https://www.anneapplebaum.com/2021/06/09/the-oligarchs-who-turn-democracy-into-something-else/.

———. *Twilight of Democracy: The Seductive Lure of Authoritarianism*. London: Vintage, 2020.

Appelbaum, Yoni. "I Alone Can Fix It." *Atlantic*, July 21, 2016. https://www.theatlantic.com/politics/archive/2016/07/trump-rnc-speech-alone-fix-it/492557/.

Armstrong, O. K., and Marjorie Armstrong. *The Baptists in America*. Garden City, NY: Doubleday, 1979.

Asher, Abe. "Trump Unleashes on 'Woke Military' and Says America Is 'Going to Hell' in Bizarre Rant." *Independent*, June 9, 2023. https://www.independent.co.uk/news/world/americas/us-politics/trump-indicted-truth-social-video-b2354498.html.

Associated Press. "Blaze Starr, Dancer Linked to Louisiana Governor Earl Long, Dead at 83." *Chicago Tribune*, June 23, 2019. https://www.chicagotribune.com/2015/06/16/blaze-starr-dancer-linked-to-louisiana-governor-earl-long-dead-at-83/.

Bacon, Percy, Jr. "Why Trump's First Moves in Office Have Been So Scary." *Washington Post*, Jan. 28, 2025. https://www.washingtonpost.com/opinions/2025/01/28/trump-first-week-liberalism-democracy/.

Bahadur, Nina. "22 Sexist Things President Donald Trump Has Said About Women." Self, June 29, 2017. https://www.self.com/story/sexist-president-donald-trump-comments.

Bahney, Jennifer Bowers. "Chris Christie Tells Trump Anecdote to Show President Trump Is Either 'A Liar or an Idiot.'" Mediaite, June 23, 2023. https://www.mediaite.com/politics/chris-christie-tells-trump-anecdote-to-show-former-president-is-either-a-liar-or-an-idiot/.

Baker, Peter. "How Trump Has Reshaped the Presidency, and How It's Changed Him, Too." *New York Times*, Apr. 29, 2017. https://www.nytimes.com/2017/04/29/us/politics/trump-presidency-100-days.html.

Bartiromo, Maria. "Interview: Maria Bartiromo of Fox Business Interviews Donald Trump." Roll Call, Oct. 13, 2024. https://rollcall.com/factbase/trump/transcript/donald-trump-interview-maria-bartiromo-fox-business-october-13-2024/.

Bassett, Laura. "Sen. Josh Hawley Shares His Mindblowingly Stupid Thoughts on Juneteenth." Jezebel, June 19, 2023. https://www.jezebel.com/sen-josh-hawley-shares-his-mindblowingly-stupid-though-1850553959.

Bates, Katharine Lee. "America the Beautiful." 1893. Hymnary.org. https://hymnary.org/text/o_beautiful_for_spacious_skies.

Bennett, Jessica. "Stormy Daniels and the Comeuppance of Donald Trump." *New York Times*, Apr. 14, 2024. https://www.nytimes.com/2024/04/14/opinion/trump-trial-stormy-daniels.html.

———. "They Call Themselves the 'Strange Sorority.' Trump Was Their Initiation." *New York Times*, Sept. 27, 2024. https://www.nytimes.com/2024/09/27/opinion/trump-accusers-stoynoff.html.

Beutler, Brian. "Why the Media Is Botching the Election." *New Republic*, Sept. 13, 2016. https://newrepublic.com/article/136730/media-botching-election.

Blanchet, Ben. "Trump Calls on Supporters to Stop 'Bags of Crap' Who Enter Polling Places." Huffington Post, Jan. 6, 2024. https://www.huffpost.com/entry/trump-supporters-stop-bags-of-crap-voting_n_6598f4bde4b0f9f6621cc828.

Blight, David. "Trump Has Birthed a Dangerous New 'Lost Cause' Myth." Gilder Lehrman Center for International and Area Studies at Yale., Jan. 13, 2022. https://macmillan.yale.edu/glc/stories/trump-has-birthed-dangerous-new-lost-cause-myth-we-must-fight-it.

Brenan, Megan. "Americans' Trust in Media Remains at Trend Low." Gallup, Oct. 14, 2024. https://news.gallup.com/poll/651977/americans-trust-media-remains-trend-low.aspx.

Bridges, Tyler. "Edwin Edwards, Louisiana Populist Who Served 4 Terms as Governor and 8 Years in Prison, Dies at 93." *Baton Rouge Advocate*, July 12, 2021. https://www.theadvocate.com/baton_rouge/news/politics/edwin-edwards-louisiana-populist-who-served-4-terms-as-governor-and-8-years-in-prison/article_6c91c6a0-2bf2-11e9-b57a-0f28036ae840.html.

Buchanan, Patrick J. *State of Emergency: The Third World Invasion and Conquest of America*. New York: Macmillan, 2007.

Budde, Marianne. "Inauguration Prayer Service Sermon Manuscript." *New Republic*, Jan. 22, 2025. https://newrepublic.com/search?search=bishop%20budde%20sermon%20transcript.

Bueno, Antoinette. "Donald Trump Says Heidi Klum 'Is No Longer a 10'—See Her Amazing Response!" Entertainment Tonight, Aug. 17, 2015. https://www.etonline.com/news/170120_donald_trump_disses_heidi_klum.

Buetler, Brian. "This Single Concept Explains Trump's Many Outrages." *New Republic*, Nov. 23, 2016. https://newrepublic.com/article/138975/single-concept-explains-trumps-many-outrages.

———. "Why the Media Is Botching the Election." *New Republic*, Sept. 13, 2016. https://newrepublic.com/article/136730/media-botching-election.

Burke, Denny (@DennyBurke). "The preacher admonishing the president is a false teacher who has no authority or right to speak." X, Jan 21, 2025. https://x.com/DennyBurk/status/1881798379107414232.

Burke, Kenneth. "The Rhetoric of Hitler's 'Battle.'" In *The Philosophy of Literary Form*. Baton Rouge: Louisiana State University Press, 1941.

Burmese American Community Institute. "Burmese Population in the USA." Aug. 4, 2023. https://thebaci.org/2023/08/04/burmese-population-in-the-usa/.

Campbell, Will D. *Soul Among Lions*. Louisville: Westminster John Knox. 1999.

Capitol News Bureau. "22 Edwin Edwards Quotes That Capture His Self-confidence and Sharp Wit." *Advocate*, July 12, 2021. https://www.theadvocate.com/baton_rouge/news/politics/22-edwin-edwards-quotes-that-capture-his-self-confidence-and-sharp-wit/article_doc60dce-e361-11eb-892c-bb2d8b75db9d.html.

Carusone, Angelo. "Donald Trump Hired Paid Actors to Attend Presidential Launch Event." Medium, June 16, 2015. https://medium.com/@GoAngelo/donald-trump-hired-paid-actors-to-attend-presidential-launch-event-7c65e8fadea0#.nzz3nj2f4.

Carville, James, and Albert Hunt. "Death of a Legend: Louisiana's Edwin Edwards Didn't Stoop to Racism." *Hill*, July 16, 2021. https://thehill.com/opinion/campaign/563336-death-of-a-legend-louisianas-edwin-edwards-didnt-stoop-to-racism/.

CBS Austin. "Dallas Pastor Calls Trump Christian 'Warrior,' Says Dems Worship Pagan God Moloch." CBS Austin, Oct. 2, 2019. https://cbsaustin.com/news/local/dallas-pastor-calls-trump-christian-warrior-says-dems-worship-pagan-god-moloch.

CBS News. "Amnesty Calls Guantanamo a 'Gulag.'" May 25, 2005. https://www.cbsnews.com/news/amnesty-calls-guantanamo-a-gulag/.

———. "Liz Cheney Tells 'CBS News Sunday Morning' That the U.S. Is 'Sleepwalking into a Dictatorship.'" Dec. 1, 2023. https://www.cbsnews.com/news/liz-cheney-tells-cbs-news-sunday-morning-that-the-u-s-is-sleepwalking-into-a-dictatorship/.

Center for American Political Studies. "Harvard CAPS Harris Poll." Dec. 2023. https://harvardharrispoll.com/wp-content/uploads/2023/12/HHP_Dec23_KeyResults.pdf.

Chalfant, Morgan. "Trump Claims He Has Done More for the Black Community than Any President Since Lincoln." *Hill*, June 6, 2020. https://thehill.com/homenews/administration/500744-trump-claims-he-has-done-more-for-black-community-than-any-president/.

Chapman, Matthew. "'You're a Lapdog': Mike Johnson Slammed over 'Shameful' Attack on Bishop." Raw Story, Jan. 22, 2025. https://www.rawstory.com/mike-johnson-bishop/.

Charlton Corey. "Married Donald Trump Said He 'Wanted to "F***" Former Playboy Model Contestant and He Repeatedly Asked Her to Marry Him During Celebrity Apprentice Filming." *Sun*, Oct. 27, 2016. https://www.thesun.co.uk/news/2059170/married-donald-trump-said-he-wanted-to-f-former-playboy-model-contestant-and-he-repeatedly-asked-to-her-marry-him-during-celebrity-apprentice-filming/.

Chouraqui, Andre. "Introduction to the Psalms." *Liturgy O.C.S.O. Journal of Gethsemani Abbey* 13 (1979) 3–29. https://cdm16259.contentdm.oclc.org/digital/collection/p15032coll3/id/56/rec/36.

Church, Francis Pharcellus. "Is There a Santa Claus?" *Sun*, Sept. 21, 1897. https://en.wikipedia.org/wiki/Yes,_Virginia,_there_is_a_Santa_Claus.

Churchill, Winston. "The Munich Agreement." Speech to the House of Commons delivered on Oct. 5, 1938. International Churchill Society. https://winstonchurchill.org/resources/speeches/1930-938-the-wilderness/the-munich-agreement/.

CNN. "President: Louisiana General Election Results." Nov. 7, 2024. https://www.cnn.com/election/2024/results/louisiana/president.

Coates, Ta-Nehisi. "The First White President." *Atlantic*, Oct. 2017. https://www.theatlantic.com/magazine/archive/2017/10/the-first-white-president-ta-nehisi-coates/537909/.

Coffin, William Sloane. *Credo*. New York: Westminster John Knox, 2004.

Cohen, Nate. "How Much Is Biden's Support of Israel Hurting Him with Young Voters?" *New York Times*, Dec. 19, 2023. https://www.nytimes.com/2023/12/19/upshot/poll-biden-trump-israel-youth.html.

Collins, Mike (@RepMikeCollins). "The person giving this sermon should be added to the deportation list." X, Jan. 21, 2025. https://x.com/RepMikeCollins/status/1881765967338131546?lang=en.

Concepcion, Summer. "Trump Says Harris Would Be 'Like a Play Toy' to World Leaders if Elected." NBC News, July 31, 2024. https://www.nbcnews.com/politics/2024-election/trump-says-harris-play-toy-world-leaders-elected-rcna164483.

Concha, Joe. "MSNBC President: Ratings on Rise Because We Give Smartest Coverage Out There." *Hill*, Mar. 3, 2017. https://thehill.com/homenews/media/322003-msnbc-president-ratings-on-rise-because-we-give-smartest-coverage-out-there/.

Cosper, Mike (@MikeCosper). "This is amazing. Won't denounce Nazis because denouncement itself is left coded." X, Jan. 21, 2025. https://x.com/MikeCosper/status/1883672271912304914.

Cotton, Tom. "Cotton Speaks Against the PRESS Act." Press Release on Tom Cotton website, Dec. 14, 2022. https://www.cotton.senate.gov/news/speeches/cotton-speaks-against-the-press-act.

Couch, Aaron, and Emmet McDermott. "Donald Trump Campaign Offered Actors $50 to Cheer for Him at Presidential Announcement." *Hollywood Reporter*, June 17, 2015. https://www.holly-woodreporter.com/news/donald-trump-campaign-offered-actors-803161.

Crane, Emily. "Elon Musk Rips Those Who Accused Him of Giving Nazi Salute: 'Need Better Dirty Tricks.'" *New York Post*, Jan. 21, 2025. https://nypost.com/2025/01/21/us-news/elon-musk-rips-those-saying-he-gave-nazi-salute-need-better-dirty-tricks/.

Daher, Natalie. "Trump Says He Doesn't Mind if a Shooter Takes Aim at 'Fake News' to Get Him." Axios, Nov. 3, 2024. https://www.axios.com/2024/11/03/trump-pennsylvania-rally-media-shooting.

Davis, Ellen F., and Richard B. Hays, eds. *The Art of Reading Scripture*. New York: Eerdmans, 2003.

Dias, Elizabeth. "The Far-Right Christian Quest for Power: 'We Are Seeing Them Emboldened.'" *New York Times*, June 22, 2023. https://www.nytimes.com/2022/07/08/us/christian-nationalism-politicians.html.

Dorman, John L. "NYT's Maggie Haberman Says Trump Gave a 'Menacing' Stare in His Mugshot Because He 'Doesn't Want to Look Weak.'" Business Insider Africa, Aug. 27, 2023. https://africa.businessinsider.com/politics/nyts-maggie-haberman-says-trump-gave-a-menacing-stare-in-his-mugshot-because-he/eyfkor3.

Dow, Bonnie J. "Taking Trump Seriously: Persona and Presidential Politics in 2016." *Women's Studies in Communication* 40 (2017) 136–39. https://doi.org/10.1080/07491409.2017.1302258.

Duggal, Hanna. "The Rise of Germany's Far-Right AfD Party." Aljazeera, Feb. 25, 2025. https://www.aljazeera.com/news/2025/2/24/charting-the-rise-of-germanys-far-right-afd-party.

Economist. "One in Five Young Americans Thinks the Holocaust Is a Myth." Dec. 7, 2023. https://www.economist.com/united-states/2023/12/07/one-in-five-young-americans-thinks-the-holocaust-is-a-myth.

Edelman, Adam. "Trump Calls Stormy Daniels Horseface After Judge Dismisses Her Suit." NBC News, Oct. 16, 2018. https://www.nbcnews.com/politics/donald-trump/trump-calls-stormy-daniels-horseface-after-judge-dismisses-her-suit-n920701.

Eksi, Betul, and Elizabeth A. Wood. "Right-Wing Populism as Gendered Performance: Janus-Faced Masculinity in the Leadership of Vladimir Putin and Recep T. Erdogan." *Theory and Society* 48 (2019) 733–51. https://www.jstor.org/stable/45219741.

Fea, John. *Believe Me: The Evangelical Road to Donald Trump*. Grand Rapids: Eerdmans, 2018.

———. "How Dare This Demonic 'Priestess' Speak Truth to Trump! (And Other Things Evangelicals Are Saying in the Wake of the Inauguration)." Way of Improvement (blog), Jan. 21, 2025. https://thewayofimprovement.blog/2025/1/21/how-dare-this-demonic-priestess-speak-truth-to-trump-and-other-things-evangelicals-are-saying-in-the-wake-of-the-inauguration/.

Filipkowski, Ron (@RonFilipowski). "Dementia Trump is riffing on his magnets in water story." X, Jan. 5, 2024. https://x.com/RonFilipkowski/status/1743473561837179153.

Folk, Zachary. "Trump Calls Walz 'Tampon Tim' in Truth Social Insult Spree." Daily Beast, Oct. 1, 2024. https://www.thedailybeast.com/trump-rages-at-tim-walz-and-cbs-moderators-minutes-into-vice-presidential-debate/.

Fortinsky, Sarah. "Pence Calls Trump's Abortion Stance a Slap in the Face to Supporters." *Hill*, Apr. 8, 2024. https://thehill.com/homenews/campaign/4581182-pence-calls-trumps-abortion-stance-a-slap-in-the-face-to-supporters/.

Fosdick, Harry Emerson. "Shall the Fundamentalists Win?" May 21, 1922. https://www.wrs.edu/assets/docs/Courses/Classic_Fundamentalism/Fosdick—Shall_Fundamentalists_Win.pdf.

Franklin, Jentezen (@Jentezen). "Always an honor to pray for @RealDonaldTrump." Instagram video, Oct. 28, 2024. https://www.instagram.com/reel/DBsN7ovIvBk/?hl=en.

French, Nancy. "Dear Pro-Lifers who are overlooking Donald Trump's sex abuse conviction." Facebook, Aug. 23, 2024. https://www.facebook.com/story.php/?story_fbid=1060365185488556&id=100045452533557.

Frum, David. "An Exit from Trumpocracy." *Atlantic*, Jan. 18, 2018. https://www.theatlantic.com/politics/archive/2018/01/frum-trumpocracy/550685/.

Granieri, Susanna. "Trump Proposal to Target Non-Citizens for Deportation on the Basis of Their Speech Is Unconsitutional, Knight Institute Says." Knight First Amendment Institute, Mar. 3, 2025. https://knightcolumbia.org/content/trump-proposal-to-target-non-citizens-for-deportation-on-the-basis-of-their-speech-is-unconstitutional-knight-institute-says.

Gregorian, Dareh. "DGOP State Legislator Opposed to Free School Lunch Proposal Says He's Never Met a Hungry Minnesotan." NBC News, Mar. 14, 2023. https://www.nbcnews.com/politics/politics-news/state-gop-senator-says-never-met-hungry-minnesotan-rcna74969.

Grossman, James. "James Baldwin on History." Perspectives on History, Aug. 3, 2016. https://www.historians.org/perspectives-article/james-baldwin-on-history-september-2016/.

Gunn, Joshua. Political Perversion: Rhetorical Aberration in the Time of Trumpeteering. Chicago: University of Chicago Press, 2020.

Haidt, Jonathan. "Why the Past Ten Years of American Life Have Been Uniquely Stupid." Atlantic, Apr. 22, 2022. https://www.theatlantic.com/magazine/archive/2022/05/social-media-democracy-trust-babel/629369/.

Halevi, Yossi Klein. "Netanyahu's Betrayal of Democracy Is a Betrayal of Israel." Atlantic, Jan. 12, 2023. https://www.theatlantic.com/ideas/archive/2023/01/benjamin-netanyahu-coalition-israel-democracy/672693/.

Hall, Colby. "Joe Scarborough Rips Marjorie Taylor Greene's 'Shameless' Effort to Expunge Trump Impeachments: 'Just So Stupid.'" Mediaite, June 23, 2023. https://www.mediaite.com/media/tv/shameless-joe-scarborough-rips-marjorie-taylor-greene-led-gesture-to-expunge-trump-impeachments-its-just-so-stupid/.

Haner, Joanne. "Walz: Trump 'Crossed a Line' with Threat to Use Military on 'Enemy from Within.'" Hill, Oct. 14, 2024. https://thehill.com/homenews/4933117-trump-military-enemy-within/.

Hart, Roderick P. Trump and Us: What He Says and Why People Listen. Cambridge: Cambridge University Press, 2020.

Hartig, Hannah, et al. "Behind Trump's 2024 Victory, a More Racially and Ethnically Diverse Voter Coalition." Pew Research Center, June 26, 2025. https://www.pewresearch.org/politics/2025/06/26/behind-trumps-2024-victory-a-more-racially-and-ethnically-diverse-voter-coalition/.

Hassel, Jeremiah. "Deranged Donald Trump Posts Mad 184-Word Easter Message Taking Aim at All His Enemies." MSN, Apr. 20, 2025. https://www.msn.com/en-us/news/opinion/deranged-donald-trump-posts-myoutubead-184-word-easter-message-taking-aim-at-all-his-enemies/ar-AA1DgJKU.

Hauerwas, Stanley. Working with Words: On Learning to Speak Christian. Eugene, OR: Cascade, 2014.

Havel, Vaclav. The Power of the Powerless: Citizens Against the State in Central-Eastern Europe. London: Routledge, 2009.

Hawhee, Debra. Moving Bodies: Kenneth Burke at the Edges of Language. Columbia: University of South Carolina Press, 2009.

Heller, Jill. "Donald Trump Calls Arianna Huffington Ugly, Cites Her Unattractiveness for Losing Her Husband." International Business Times, Aug. 28, 2012. https://www.ibtimes.com/donald-trump-calls-arianna-huffington-ugly-cites-her-unattractiveness-losing-her-husband-759517.

Holling, Michelle A., and Dreama G. Moon. "20/20 in 2020?: Refractive Vision, 45, and White Supremacy." *Quarterly Journal of Speech* 107 (2021) 435–42. https://doi.org /10.1080/00335630.2021.1983195.

Howe, Julia Ward. "The Battle Hymn of the Republic." Poetry Foundation. https://www. poetryfoundation.org/poems/44420/battle-hymn-of-the-republic.

Iafrate, Anthony. "Why Harris Lost: The Democrats Exiled Young Male Voters in Favor of the Political Class." Catholic Vote, Nov. 17, 2024. https://catholicvote.org/why-harris-lost-the-democrats-exiled-young-male-voters-in-favor-of-the-political-class/.

Ibssa, Lalee, and Soo Rim Kim. "Trump Boasts of Role Ending Roe v. Wade." ABC News, Jan. 10, 2024. https://abcnews.go.com/Politics/trump-boasts-role-ending-roe-wade-abortion-regulations/story?id=106280890.

International Holocaust Remembrance Alliance. "Working Definition of Antisemitism." https://holocaustremembrance.com/resources/working-definition-antisemitism.

Irwin, Lauren. "Cotton Blocks Federal Shield Law for Journalists." *Hill*, Dec. 10, 2024. https://thehill.com/homenews/senate/5033592-cotton-blocks-federal-shield-law-journalists/.

Ivie, Robert L. "Dissenting Democratically from Trump's Toxic Tropes." *Javnost - The Public* 30 (2023) 1–17.

———. "Enabling Democratic Dissent." *Quarterly Journal of Speech* 101 (2015) 46–59.

———. "Trump's Unwitting Prophecy." *Rhetoric and Public Affairs* 20 (2017) 707–18.

Jacobson, Louis. "Donald Trump Said He's Done More for African Americans than Any President. Historians Disagree." Politico, Aug. 1, 2019. https://www.politifact.com/ article/2019/aug/01/donald-trump-said-hes-done-more-african-americans-/.

———. "Fact-Checking Donald Trump's Tweet Saying Democrats 'Don't Mind Executing' Babies After Birth." PolitiFact, Feb. 28, 2019. https://www.politifact. com/factchecks/2019/feb/28/donald-trump/fact-checking-donald-trumps-tweet-saying-democrats/.

Jacobson, Louis, et al. "Trump's False Crowd Comparison with His Jan. 6 Speech and the Crowd at MLK's 'I Have a Dream' Speech." Politifact, Aug. 9, 2024. https:// www.politifact.com/factchecks/2024/aug/09/donald-trump/trumps-false-mlk-speech-jan-6-crowd-size/.

Jane, Talia. "Cognitive Decline? Trump Brags About Putting His Pants on by Himself." *New Republic*, May 24, 2024. https://newrepublic.com/post/181922/trump-brags-pants-bronx-rally.

Janfaza, Rachel. "We Asked Young Men Why They Voted for Donald Trump." *Glamour*, Nov. 15, 2024. https://www.glamour.com/story/why-did-young-men-vote-for-donald-trump.

Jefferson, Thomas. "Thomas Jefferson to Charles Yancey, 6 January 1816." National Archives. https://founders.archives.gov/documents/Jefferson/03-09-02-0209.

———. "Thomas Jefferson to James Currie, 28 January 1786." National Archives. https://founders.archives.gov/documents/Jefferson/01-09-02-0209.

Jeffress, Robert. *Twilight's Last Gleaming: How America's Last Days Can Be Your Best Days*. New York: Worthy, 2012.

——— (@Jeffress). "Attended national prayer service today at the Washington National Cathedral." X, Jan. 21, 2025. https://x.com/robertjeffress/status/1881798007340900459.

———— (@Jeffress). "@POTUS is doing more to celebrate the true meaning of Easter than any president in history!" X, Apr. 16, 2025. https://x.com/robertjeffress/status/1912553801522765863.

Jewish Chronicle. "Nearly Half of Americans Can't Name a Single Nazi Death Camp, New Study Finds." Jan. 23, 2025. https://www.thejc.com/news/americans-nazi-death-camp-holocaust-survey-r28yh1i1.

Johnson, Paul Elliott. "The Art of Masculine Victimhood: Donald Trump's Demagoguery." Women's Studies in Communication 40 (2017) 229–50.

Jones, Terry, dir. Monty Python's Life of Brian. London: Cinema International, 1979. https://youtu.be/QereRoCViMY.

Kaczynski, Andrew. "Mike Huckabee Once Said That 'There's Really No Such Thing as a Palestinian.'" CNN, Nov. 12, 2024. https://www.cnn.com/2024/11/12/politics/mike-huckabee-palestinian-comments-trump-israel-ambassador.

Kaplan, Rebecca. "Donald Trump: 'I Will Be Phenomenal to the Women.'" CBS News, Aug. 9, 2015. https://www.cbsnews.com/news/donald-trump-i-will-be-phenomenal-to-the-women/.

Kelly, Casey Ryan. "Donald J. Trump and the Rhetoric of Ressentiment." Quarterly Journal of Speech 106 (2020) 2–24.

Kelly, Laura. "Trump: 'All Hell Will Break Out.'" Hill, Nov. 17, 2024. https://thehill.com/policy/international/5071625-trump-warns-hostage-release/.

Kennedy, Rodney. Good and Evil in the Garden of Democracy. Eugene, OR: Cascade, 2023.

————. The Immaculate Mistake: How Evangelicals Gave Birth to Donald Trump. Eugene, OR: Cascade, 2021.

Ketchin, Susan. The Christ-Haunted Landscape: Faith and Doubt in Southern Fiction. Jackson: University Press of Mississippi, 2009.

Kierkegaard, Søren. The Journal of Kierkegaard. Translated and selected with an introduction by Alexander Dru. New York: Harper & Row, 1958.

Kika, Thomas. "Donald Trump Ridiculed for Bizarre Magnet Remarks at Iowa Rally." Newsweek, Jan. 6, 2024. https://www.newsweek.com/donald-trump-ridiculed-bizarre-magnet-remarks-iowa-rally-1858420.

Klaas, Brian. "Trump Rants About Sharks and Everyone Just Pretends Its Normal." Atlantic, June 12, 2024. https://www.theatlantic.com/politics/archive/2024/06/trump-shark-rant/678666/.

Klein, Camilla. "How Much Does The Average Christian Give To Church?" Christian Educators Academy, Oct. 18, 2024. https://christianeducatorsacademy.com/how-much-does-the-average-christian-give-to-church/.

Kloppenberg, James T. Toward Democracy: The Struggle for Self-Rule in European and American Thought. Oxford: Oxford University Press, 2016.

Kramer, Stephanie. "Religion in North America." Pew Research Center, June 9, 2025. https://www.pewresearch.org/religion/2025/06/09/religion-in-north-america/.

Kruse, Kevin M. One Nation Under God: How Corporate America Invented Christian America. New York: Basic, 2015.

Lakoff, George. The Political Mind: Why You Can't Understand 21st-Century Politics with an 18th-Century Brain. New York: Penguin, 2008.

Lazarus, Emma. "The New Colossus." 1903. Poetry Foundation. https://www.poetryfoundation.org/poems/46550/the-new-colossus.

Lebowitz, Megan, and Jake Traylor. "Trump Compares Migrants to Hannibal Lecter in 'The Silence of the Lambs.'" NBC News, Mar. 4, 2024. https://www.nbcnews.com/politics/donald-trump/trump-compares-migrants-hannibal-lecter-silence-lambs-rcna141792.

Lee, Jasmine C., and Kevin Quealy. "The 598 People, Places and Things Donald Trump Has Insulted on Twitter: A Complete List." *New York Times*, May 24, 2019. https://www.nytimes.com/interactive/2016/01/28/upshot/donald-trump-twitter-insults.html.

Leeson, Lucy. "Donald Trump Bizarrely Claims Migrants Have Phone App Direct to Kamala Harris." *Independent*, Sept. 20, 2024. https://www.independent.co.uk/tv/news/donald-trump-immigration-phone-app-kamala-harris-b2619755.html.

Leibovich, Mark. "The Tipping Point of Stupid." Taegan Goddard's Political Wire, Sept. 22, 2022. https://politicalwire.com/2022/09/22/the-tipping-point-of-stupid/.

Leland, John. *The Writings of John Leland*. Edited by L. F. Greene. 1845. Repr., New York: Amo, 1969.

Leonard, Bill. *Baptist Ways: A History*. Valley Forge, PA: Judson. 2003.

Lindsay, James M. "With the Electoral College Votes Now Cast, Here Is a Recap of How Americans Voted in 2024." Council on Foreign Relations, Dec. 18, 2024. https://www.cfr.org/article/2024-election-numbers.

Liquisearch. "Edwin Edwards—A Second Comeback: Edwards vs. Duke, 1991." https://www.liquisearch.com/edwin_edwards/a_second_comeback_-_edwards_vs_duke_1991.

Litman, Harry. "What Kind of Prosecutor Was Kamala Harris? The Answer Could Be Pivotal to Her Campaign." TribLive, Aug. 23, 2024. https://triblive.com/opinion/harry-litman-what-kind-of-prosecutor-was-kamala-harris-the-answer-could-be-pivotal-to-her-campaign/.

Lyons, Julie. "Robert Jeffress Wants a 'Mean Son of a Gun' for President." *Dallas Observer*, Apr. 15, 2016. https://www.dallasobserver.com/news/robert-jeffress-wants-a-mean-son-of-a-gun-for-president-says-trump-isnt-a-racist-8184721.

Maginnis, John. "The Last Populist: Ed Edwards' Graceful Goodbye to Louisiana Politics." *Los Angeles Times*, June 12, 1994. https://www.latimes.com/archives/la-xpm-1994-96-12-op-3169-story.html.

Mallin, Alexander. "Judge Slams Trump as 'Charlatan' After Jury Finds Jan. 6 Rioter Guilty on All Counts." ABC News, Apr. 14, 2022. https://abcnews.go.com/Politics/judge-slams-trump-charlatan-jury-finds-jan-rioter/story?id=84090253.

Marcotte, Amanda. "'Too Stupid to Know Better': MAGA Eats Up Trump's Idiot President Defense." Salon, June 21, 2023. https://www.salon.com/2023/06/21/too-stupid-to-know-better-maga-eats-up-idiot-defense/.

Matthews, Dylan. "Read Every Horrible Thing Donald Trump Has Said About Women and Tell Me He's Not a Sexist." *Vox*, May 16, 2016. https://www.vox.com/2016/5/16/11683122/donald-trump-misogynist-sexist.

Mazza, Ed. "'Dimbulb' Trump Torched After Rambling Attempt to Explain Gettysburg Goes Wrong." HuffPost, Apr. 15, 2024. https://www.huffpost.com/entry/donald-trump-gettysburg_n_661c975be4b0f8e522daf77f.

———. "Trump's Absolutely Baffling Claim About 'Phone Apps' Raises New Questions." HuffPost, Sept. 30, 2024. https://www.msn.com/en-us/news/politics/trumps-absolutely-baffling-claim-about-phone-apps-raises-new-questions/ar-AA1rsjuP.

McAdams, Dan P. "The Mind of Donald Trump." *Atlantic*, June, 2016. https://www. theatlantic.com/magazine/archive/2016/06/the-mind-of-donald-trump/480771/.

McElvaine, Robert S. *The Great Depression: America 1929–1941*. New York: Crown, 1993. Kindle.

McFadden, Robert D. "Edwin Edwards, Flamboyant Louisiana Governor, Is Dead at 93." *New York Times*, July 12, 2021. https://www.nytimes.com/2021/07/12/us/politics/edwin-edwards-dead.html.

McGaughy, Lauren. "Edwin Edwards' Best Quotes: A Look Back as We Look Ahead to His Congressional Run." *Times Picayune*, Mar. 17, 2014. https://www.nola.com/news/politics/edwin-edwards-best-quotes-a-look-back-as-we-look-ahead-to-his-congressional-run/article_baa97da0–8d95–5c6a-8d3b-9feobbebc216.html.

McGee, Heather. *The Sum of Us: What Racism Costs Everyone and How We Can Prosper Together*. New York: One World, 2021.

McKay, Tom. "15 Head-Scratching Quotes from Donald Trump's Presidential Announcement Speech." Mic, June 16, 2015. https://mic.com/articles/120785/best-quotes-from-donald-trumps-2016-presidential-announcement-speech#.4Ukn1Nojd.

McMenamin, Michael. "Action This Day Summer 1886, 1911, 1936, 1961." International Churchill Society, May 5, 2013. https://winstonchurchill.org/publications/finest-hour/finest-hour-151/action-this-day-summer-1886-1911-1936-1961/.

McShane, Julianne. "Press Freedom Groups Warn of the Threat Posed by Trump." Mother Jones, Nov. 10, 2024. https://www.motherjones.com/politics/2024/11/press-freedom-groups-trump-threat/.

Mercieca, Jennifer. *Demagogue for President: The Rhetorical Genius of Donald Trump*. College Station: Texas A&M University Press, 2020.

Milbank, Dana. "The GOP Is Sick: It Didn't Start with Trump and Won't End with Him." *Washington Post*, Aug. 4, 2022. https://www.washingtonpost.com/opinions/2022/08/04/dana-milbank-republican-destructionists-book-excerpt/.

Miles, Frank. "Trump Pennsylvania Rally: President Marks First Promises Made and Kept in Office." Fox News, Apr. 29, 2017. https://www.foxnews.com/politics/trump-pennsylvania-rally-president-marks-first-promises-made-and-kept-in-office?msockid=30699c9b655c61a33585898d6427608d.

Miller, Julie. "Revisit the Time Donald Trump Said Kim Kardashian Had 'Gotten a Bit Large.'" Vanity Fair, Sept. 28, 2016. https://www.vanityfair.com/style/2016/09/kim-kardashian-donald-trump-body-shaming.

Mindock, Clark. "Donald Trump to Emmanuel Macron's Wife Brigitte: 'You Know, You're in Such Great Shape . . . Beautiful.'" *Independent*, July 13, 2017. https://www.independent.co.uk/news/world/americas/us-politics/trump-macron-wife-brigitte-comments-great-shape-beautiful-france-first-lady-a7840076.html.

Mitchell, Margaret Mary. *The Heavenly Trumpet: John Chrysostom and the Art of Pauline Interpretation*. Hermeneutische Untersuchungen zur Theologie 40. Louisville: Westminster John Knox Press, 2002.

Montanaro, Domenico. "162 Lies and Distortions in a News Conference. NPR Fact-Checks Former President Trump." NPR, Aug. 11, 2024. https://www.npr.org/2024/08/11/nx-s1-5070566/trump-news-conference.

Montgomery, Peter. "Trump Tells Christian Nationalist Leaders the U.S. Will Be Better Off When He's Given Them More Power." Right Wing Watch, Oct. 29, 2024. https://www.peoplefor.org/rightwingwatch/trump-tells-christian-nationalist-leaders-us-will-be-better-when-hes-given-them-more.

Montoya-Galvez, Camilo. "Pelosi Questions Trump's Manhood, Compares Him to a Skunk After Oval Office Clash." CBS News, Dec. 11, 2018. https://www.cbsnews.com/news/pelosi-questions-trumps-manhood-compares-him-to-a-skunk-after-oval-office-clash/.

Murphy, Chad. "The Truth About Springfield, Ohio: Are Immigrants Eating Dogs as Trump Says? What to Know." *Columbus Dispatch*, Sept. 11, 2024. https://www.dispatch.com/story/news/2024/09/11/truth-fact-check-people-eating-dogs-springfield-ohio-trump-vance-harris-debate/75171964007/.

Naylor, Brian. "Read Trump's Jan. 6 Speech, a Key Part of Impeachment Trial." NPR, Feb. 10, 2021. https://www.npr.org/2021/02/10/966396848/read-trumps-jan-6-speech-a-key-part-of-impeachment-trial.

NBC News. "Elon Musk Tells German Crowd to Be Proud and Move Beyond the 'Sins of Their Parents' During Video Appearance at Far Right Event." Reuters, Jan. 25, 2025. https://www.nbcnews.com/news/world/elon-musk-far-right-germans-proud-past-sins-rcna189281.

Neath, Amelia. "Trump Shares Bizarre Court Sketch of Him Sitting next to Jesus at Civil Fraud Trial." *Independent*, Oct. 3, 2023. https://www.independent.co.uk/news/world/americas/us-politics/trump-court-sketch-jesus-christ-b2423039.html.

Neukam, Stephen. "Trump Opens Campaign Rally with Song Featuring Jan. 6 Defendants." *Hill*, Mar. 23, 2016. https://thehill.com/homenews/campaign/3918877-trump-opens-campaign-rally-with-song-featuring-jan-6-defendants/.

Nieto, Phillip. "Trump Posts Shockingly Crass Comment About Kamala Harris, Hillary Clinton and 'Blowjobs.'" Mediate, Aug. 28, 2024. https://www.mediaite.com/politics/trump/trump-posts-shockingly-crass-comment-about-kamala-harris-hillary-clinton-and-blowjobs/.

NPR. "Read Trump's Jan. 6 Speech, a Key Part of Impeachment Trial." Feb. 10, 2021. https://www.npr.org/2021/02/10/966396848/read-trumps-jan-6-speech-a-key-part-of-impeachment-trial.

———. "Trump Threatens to Use the Military and DOJ to Go After Those Who Are Disloyal." Oct. 21, 2024. https://www.npr.org/2024/10/21/nx-s1-5155005/trump-threatens-to-use-the-military-and-doj-to-go-after-those-who-are-disloyal.

O'Connor, Flannery. *Wise Blood*. New York: Macmillan, 1952. Kindle.

Oppenheim, May. "Donald Trump Says You Have to Deny, Deny, Deny." *Independent*, Sept. 12, 2018. https://www.independent.co.uk/news/world/americas/us-politics/trump-women-bob-woodward-deny-sexual-assault-stormy-daniels-book-fear-a8534061.html.

Ott, Brian L., and Greg Dickinson. *The Twitter Presidency: Donald J. Trump and the Politics of White Rage*. New York: Routledge, 2019.

Packer, George. "Hillary Clinton and the Populist Revolt." *New Yorker*, Oct. 24, 2016. https://www.newyorker.com/magazine/2016/10/31/hillary-clinton-and-the-populist-revolt.

Page, Myriam. "Trump Bizarrely Claims People Have Stopped Eating Bacon Because of Wind Power." *Independent*, Aug. 30, 2024. https://www.independent.co.uk/news/world/americas/us-politics/donald-trump-bacon-rally-wind-power-b2604316.html.

Paine, Thomas. *Rights of Man: Being an Answer to Mr. Burke's Attack on the French Revolution*. 2nd ed. London: J. S. Jordan, 1791. https://oll.libertyfund.org/titles/paine-the-rights-of-man-part-i-1791-ed.

Pelosi, Nancy. "Transcript of Pelosi Floor Speech on Future Plans." Press Release on Pelosi website, Nov. 17, 2022. https://pelosi.house.gov/news/press-releases/transcript-of-pelosi-floor-speech-on-future-plans.

Perkins, Tony (@tperkins). "The cause of America's decline was not what was sitting in the pew." X, Jan 21, 2025. https://x.com/tperkins/status/1881796957188100181.

Perry, Samuel L. "Why Evangelicals Went All In on Trump, Again." *Time*, Jan. 24, 2024. https://time.com/6588138/evangelicals-support-donald-trump-2024/.

Pettypiece, Shannon. "Marjorie Taylor Greene Calls for a 'National Divorce' Between Liberal and Conservative States." NBC News, Feb. 20, 2023. https://www.nbcnews.com/politics/congress/marjorie-taylor-greene-calls-national-divorce-liberal-conservative-sta-rcna71464.

Pfeiffer, Sacha. "Trump Wants to Send 30,000 Migrants to Guantanamo. Here Are the Hurdles." NPR, All Things Considered, Jan. 30, 2025. https://prod-www.npr.org/transcripts/.

Pius XI. *Mit Brennender Sorge.* Given at the Vatican Mar. 14, 1937. https://www.vatican.va/content/pius-xi/en/encyclicals/documents/hf_p-xi_enc_14031937_mit-brennender-sorge.html.

Plumer, Brad. "Full Transcript of Donald Trump's Acceptance Speech at the RNC." *Vox*, July 22, 2016. https://www.vox.com/2016/7/21/12253426/donald-trump-acceptance-speech-transcript-republican-nomination-transcript.

Politi, James, and Courtney Weaver. "'She Was Trump's Biggest Problem': Nancy Pelosi's Exit Marks End of an Era." *Financial Times*, Nov. 17, 2022. https://www.ft.com/content/bfa77d05-2e38-485b-94aa-fef6f971bc47.

Posetti, Julie, and Waqas Ejaz. "Ahead of US Election, Tolerance for Attacks on Journalists Is Alarmingly High." International Journalists' Network, Nov. 4, 2024. https://ijnet.org/en/story/ahead-us-election-tolerance-attacks-journalists-alarmingly-high.

Price, Michelle L., and Will Weissert. "Trump Blames Biden and Harris' Rhetoric Toward Him Despite His Own History of Going After Rivals." Associated Press, Sept. 16, 2024. https://apnews.com/article/trump-harris-2024-election-assassination-attempt-836523f3bbecf4a183dc46fbefd8230a.

Probyn, Elspeth. *Blush: Faces of Shame.* Minneapolis: University of Minnesota Press, 2005.

Prusa, Igor, and Matthew Brummer. "Myth, Fiction and Politics in the Age of Antiheroes: A Case Study of Donald Trump." *Heroism Science* 7 (2022) 1–39. https://doi.org/10.26736/hs.2022.01.10.

Puleo, Stephen. *The Caning: The Assault That Drove America to Civil War.* Yardley, PA: Westholme, 2012.

Ramirez, Nikki McCann. "Trump Rants After Felony Conviction: 'Our Whole Country Is Rigged.'" *Rolling Stone*, May 30, 2023. https://www.rollingstone.com/politics/politics-news/trump-rants-after-felony-conviction-hush-money-rigged-1235030175/.

Rappeport, Alan. "Donald Trump's Trail of Comments About Women." *New York Times*, Mar. 25, 2016. https://www.nytimes.com/2016/03/26/us/politics/donald-trump-women.html.

Rascouët-Paz, Anna. "Fact Check: Bill Clinton Said Democratic Presidents Created 50M of 51M Jobs Since 1989. We Crunched the Numbers." MSN, Sept. 10, 2024. https://www.msn.com/en-us/news/politics/fact-check-bill-clinton-said-democratic-presidents-created-50m-of-51m-jobs-since-1989-we-crunched-the-numbers/ar-AA1qk7jX.

Rauch, Jonathan. "Trump's Second Term Would Look Like This." *Atlantic*, Aug. 29, 2022. https://www.theatlantic.com/ideas/archive/2022/08/trump-2024-reelection-viktor-orban-hungary/671264/.

Raven, Julian. "The Trump Painting Unafraid and Unashamed: The First Presidential Trump Portrait 2015." https://thetrumppainting.com/.

Read, Rupert. "What Is New in Our Time: The Truth in 'Post-Truth'; A Response to Finlayson." *Nordic Wittgenstein Review* 8 (2019) 81–96.

Repucci, Sarah, and Amy Slipowitz. "Freedom in the World 2021: Democracy Under Siege." Freedom House. https://freedomhouse.org/report/freedom-world/2021/democracy-under-siege.

Reston, Maeve. "Trump Continues Bizarre Appeals to Suburban Women." CNN Politics, Oct. 18, 2020. https://www.cnn.com/2020/10/18/politics/donald-trump-women-gretchen-whitmer.

Richards, Kimberley. "A Pastor's Powerful Plea for 'Mercy' Drew Trump's Ire—And Faith Leaders Have Something to Say." HuffPost, Jan. 22, 2025. https://www.huffpost.com/entry/donald-trump-bishop-mariann-edgar-budde-faith-leaders-experts_l_6791332ae4b0835f2b833a90.

Roberts-Miller, Patricia. "Rhetoric and Hitler: An Introduction." Patricia Roberts-Miller (blog), Aug. 27, 2018. https://www.patriciarobertsmiller.com/category/hitler-and-rhetoric-fs-2018/.

Robinson, Laura (@LauraRbnsn). "I have no idea what to do with a Christian who responds to news of starving kids with celebration." X, Mar. 3, 2025. https://x.com/LauraRbnsn/status/1896592543284183528.

Rogers, Katie, and Nicholas Fandos. "Trump Tells Congresswomen to 'Go Back' to the Countries They Came From." *New York Times*, July 14. 2019. https://www.nytimes.com/2019/07/14/us/politics/trump-twitter-squad-congress.html.

Rohter, Larry. "Real Deal on 'Joe the Plumber' Reveals New Slant." *New York Times*, Oct. 16, 2008.

Roll Call. "Speech: Donald Trump Holds a Campaign Rally in Aurora, Colorado—October 11, 2024." https://rollcall.com/factbase/trump/transcript/donald-trump-speech-campaign-rally-aurora-colorado-october-11-2024/.

Roosevelt, Franklin D. "Second Inaugural Address, Jan. 20, 1937." In *Rendezvous with Destiny: Addresses and Opinions of Franklin Delano Roosevelt*, edited by J. B. S. Hardman. New York: Dryden, 1944. Repr., Whitefish, MT: Kessinger, 2005.

Samuels, Brett. "Trump Vows to Appoint Special Prosecutor to 'Go After' Biden if Former President Wins in 2024." *Hill*, June 6, 2023. https://thehill.com/homenews/campaign/4045934-trump-vows-to-appoint-special-prosecutor-to-go-after-biden-if-former-president-wins-in-2024/.

Say It Plain. "Fannie Lou Hamer (1917–1977): Testimony Before the Credentials Committee, Democratic National Convention." American Public Media. https://americanradioworks.publicradio.org/features/sayitplain/flhamer.html.

Schaefer, Donovan. "Whiteness and Civilization: Shame, Race, and the Rhetoric of Donald Trump." *Communication and Critical Studies* 7 (2020) 1–18.

Schorr, Daniel. "Joe the Plumber and the Wealth Gap." NPR, Oct. 21, 2008. https://www.npr.org/2008/10/21/95949897/joe-the-plumber-and-the-wealth-gap.

Shaw, Adam. "Trump Reveals New Pledge Amid Haitian Refugee Controversy: 'I Will Save Our Cities.'" Fox News, Sept. 16, 2024. https://www.foxnews.com/politics/trump-reveals-new-pledge-amid-haitian-refugee-controversy-save-our-cities?msockid=30699c9b655c61a33585898d6427608d.

Skinnell, Ryan. "What Passes for Truth in the Trump Era: Telling It Like It Isn't." In *Faking the News*, edited by Ryan Skinnell. Exeter: Imprint Academic, 2018.

Smith, Craig R. "Ronald Reagan's Rhetorical Re-Invention of Conservatism." *Quarterly Journal of Speech* 103 (2017) 33–65.

Smith, David Livingstone. *Less than Human: Why We Demean, Enslave, and Exterminate Others*. New York: Macmillan. 2011.

Smith, James K. A. *How (Not) to Be Secular: Reading Charles Taylor*. Grand Rapids: Eerdmans, 2014. Kindle.

Smith, Lee. *Me and My Baby View the Eclipse*. New York: Penguin, 2014.

Smith, Peter. "White Evangelical Voters Show Steadfast Support for Donald Trump's Presidency." Associated Press, Nov. 7, 2024. https://apnews.com/article/white-evangelical-voters-support-donald-trump-president-dbfd2b4fe5b2ea27968876f19ee20c84.

Snyder, Timothy. *On Tyranny Graphic Edition: Twenty Lessons from the Twentieth Century*. New York: Tim Duggan, 2021.

Southern Poverty Law Center. "Hate Map." https://www.splcenter.org/hate-map/.

Spitalnick, Amy. "JCPA Responds to Trump Administration's Executive Order on Antisemitism." Jewish Council for Public Affairs, Jan. 29, 2025. https://jewishpublicaffairs.org/news/jcpa-responds-to-trump-administrations-executive-order-on-antisemitism/.

Stack, Liam. "Donald Trump Keeps Insulting Rosie O'Donnell. Here's How Their Feud Started." *New York Times*, Sept. 28, 2016. https://www.nytimes.com/2016/09/29/us/donald-trump-keeps-insulting-rosie-odonnell-heres-how-their-feud-started.html.

Stanaland, Adam. "Why Gen Z Men Voted for Trump." *Scientific American*, Dec. 4, 2024. https://www.scientificamerican.com/article/why-gen-z-men-voted-for-trump/.

Steudeman, Michael J. "Demagoguery and the Donald's Duplicitous Claims." In *Faking the News: What Rhetoric Can Teach Us About Donald J. Trump*, edited by Ryan Skinnell. Exeter: Imprint Academic, 2018.

Stuckey, Allie Beth (@conservmillen). "How Can I still Vote for Trump?" X. Oct. 28, 2024. https://x.com/conservmillen/status/1850919179857064198.

Stuckey, Mary E. "American Elections and the Rhetoric of Political Change: Hyperbole, Anger, and Hope in U.S. Politics." *Rhetoric and Public Affairs* 20 (2017) 667–94.

Taylor, Hugh. "Should We Celebrate the Deportations of Pro-Activist Palestinians?" The Times of Israel, Jan. 31, 2025. https://blogs.timesofisrael.com/should-we-celebrate-deportations-of-pro-palestinian-activists/.

Thomson, Alice. "Bill Gates: Trump, Musk and How My Neurodiversity Made Me." *Times*, Jan. 25, 2025. https://www.thetimes.com/life-style/celebrity/article/bill-gates-interview-new-book-memoir-wh766b9bs.

Tierney, McAfee. "Donald Trump Once Boasted He Could Have 'Nailed' Princess Diana." Y!Entertainment, May 18, 2018. https://www.yahoo.com/entertainment/donald-trump-once-boasted-could-195252824.html.

Tilley, Terrence W. *The Evils of Theodicy*. Eugene, OR: Wipf & Stock, 2000.

Time Staff. "Read the Transcript of Trump's 2025 Speech to Congress Here." *Time*, Mar. 5, 2025. https://time.com/7264688/trump-speech-congress-2025-transcript/.

Trollinger, William. "*Good and Evil in the Garden of Democracy*: An Interview with Rodney Kennedy." Righting America, May 17, 2023. https://rightingamerica. net/good-and-evil-in-the-garden-of-democracy-an-interview-with-rodney-kennedy/.

———. "*The Immaculate Mistake: How Evangelicals Gave Birth to Donald Trump*; An Interview with Rodney Kennedy." Righting America, Aug. 19, 2021. https:// rightingamerica.net/the-immaculate-mistake-how-evangelicals-gave-birth-to-donald-trump-an-interview-with-rodney-kennedy/.

Trump, Donald. "Donald Trump Election Campaign Rally in Sioux Center, Iowa." Rev, Jan. 4, 2024. https://www.rev.com/transcripts/donald-trump-election-campaign-rally-in-sioux-center-iowa-transcript.

———. "Donald Trump Presidential Campaign Announcement." Broadcast on CSPAN June 16, 2015. https://archive.org/details/CSPAN3_20150616_150000_Donald_Trump_Presidential_Campaign_Announcement/.

———. "Donald Trump Rally in Philadelphia." Rev, June 22, 2024. https://www.rev. com/transcripts/donald-trump-rally-in-philadelphia.

———. "Donald Trump Rally Johnstown, PA Transcript October 13." Rev. https://www. rev.com/transcripts/donald-trump-rally-johnstown-pa-transcript-october-13.

———. "Trump Rally in Latrobe, Pennsylvania." Rev. https://www.rev.com/transcripts/ trump-rally-in-latrobe-pennsylvania.

———. "Trump Rally in Scranton, Pennsylvania." Rev, Oct. 9, 2024. https://www.rev. com/transcripts/trump-rally-in-scranton-pennsylvania.

——— (@realDonaldTrump)."I will be great for women." Truth Social, Aug. 23, 2024. https://truthsocial.com/@realDonaldTrump/posts/113012083325505976.

——— (@realDonaldTrump). "Senate Democrats just voted against legislation to prevent the killing of newborn infant children." X, Feb. 25, 2019. https://x.com/ realDonaldTrump/status/1100211495223218176.

——— (@realDonaldTrump). "She Failed to Mention the Large Number of Illegal Migrants that Came into Our Country and Killed People." Truth Social, Jan. 21, 2025.

Uchimiya, Ellen. "Trump Insults Carly Fiorina's Appearance." CBS News, Sept. 10, 2015. https://www.cbsnews.com/news/donald-trump-insults-carly-fiorinas-appearance/.

US Customs and Border Protection. "CBP Designs CBP One Mobile App to Streamline Lawful Travel to United States." Feb. 2, 2021. https://www.cbp.gov/newsroom/ national-media-release/cbp-designs-cbp-one-mobile-app-streamline-lawful-travel-united.

Vásquez, Ian, et al. *Human Freedom Index 2023: A Global Measurement of Personal, Civic, and Economic Freedom*. Washington, DC: Cato Institute and Fraser Institute, 2023.

Vischer, Phil (@philvischer). "The Trump admin sent notices on Wednesday to the Christian orgs that work to help refugees resettle in the US." X, Mar. 1, 2025. https://x.com/philvischer/status/1896062083680383483.

Walker, Chris. "Trump Tells Supporters Rallygoer Who Broke Through Press Fence Is 'On Our Side.'" Truthout, Sept. 4, 2024. https://truthout.org/articles/trump-tells-supporters-rallygoer-who-broke-through-press-fence-is-on-our-side/.

Warzel, Charlie. "Did He Actually Do That?" *Atlantic*, Jan. 20, 2025. https://www.theatlantic.com/technology/archive/2025/01/musk-trump-inauguration-salute/681390/.

Watkins, Eli. "Trump Tells Jewish Magazine's Reporter to 'Sit Down.'" CNN, Feb. 16, 2017. https://www.cnn.com/2017/02/16/politics/donald-trump-news-conference-anti-semitism/.

Watson, Kathryn, et al. "Trump Says U.S. Will Send 'Worst Criminal Illegal Aliens' to Guantanamo Bay." CBS News, Jan. 29, 2025. https://www.cbsnews.com/news/trump-executive-order-guantanamo-bay-for-criminal-migrants/.

Weisman, Jonathan, et al. "Poll Finds Wide Spread Disapproval of Biden on Gaza, and Little Room to Shift Gears." *New York Times*, Dec. 19, 2023. https://www.nytimes.com/2023/12/19/us/politics/biden-israel-gaza-poll.html.

West, Cornel. *Democracy Matters: Winning the Fight Against Imperialism*. New York: Penguin, 2005.

White, Daniel. "Donald Trump Tells Crowd to 'Knock the Crap out of' Hecklers." *Time*, Feb. 1, 2016. https://time.com/4203094/donald-trump-hecklers/.

The White House. "Fact Sheet: President Donald J. Trump Takes Forceful and Unprecedented Steps to Combat Anti-Semitism." Jan. 30, 2025. https://www.whitehouse.gov/fact-sheets/2025/01/fact-sheet-president-donald-j-trump-takes-forceful-and-unprecedented-steps-to-combat-anti-semitism/.

Whitman, Walt. *Leaves of Grass: The First Edition of 1855 and the Death Bed Edition of 1892*. E-artnow, 2013.

Williams, Roger. *The Bloudy Tenent of Persecution*. Providence, RI: Narragansett Club, 1867.

Wingard, Jennifer. "Trump's Not Just One Bad Apple: He's the Product of a Spoiled Bunch." In *Faking the News*, edited by Ryan Skinnell. Exeter: Imprint Academic, 2018.

Young, Anna. "Rhetorics of Fear and Loathing: Donald Trump's Populist Style." In *Faking the News*, edited by Ryan Skinnell. Exeter: Imprint Academic. 2018.

Young, Stephen. "A Guide to Robert Jeffress' Excuses for President Trump." *Observer*, Aug. 31, 2018. https://www.dallasobserver.com/news/robert-jeffress-top-10-excuses-for-donald-trump-11085895.

Zagacki, Kenneth S. "Vaclav Havel and the Rhetoric of Folly." *Southern Journal of Communication* 62 (1996) 17–30.